T0145661

THE
NEW WORLD
OF WORK

SECOND EDITION

THE
NEW
WORLD
OF
WORK

THE CUBE, THE CLOUD,
AND WHAT'S NEXT

TIM HOULNE & TERRI MAXWELL

 | Books

Published by Advantage, Charleston, South Carolina.
Member of Advantage Media.

ADVANTAGE is a registered trademark, and the Advantage colophon is a trademark of Advantage Media Group, Inc.

Printed in the United States of America.

10 9 8 7 6 5 4 3 2 1

ISBN: 978-1-64225-831-8 (Paperback)
ISBN: 978-1-64225-830-1 (eBook)

LCCN: 2022923921

Cover design by Wesley Strickland.
Layout design by Analisa Smith.

This publication is designed to provide accurate and authoritative information in regard to the subject matter covered. It is sold with the understanding that the publisher is not engaged in rendering legal, accounting, or other professional services. If legal advice or other expert assistance is required, the services of a competent professional person should be sought.

Advantage Media helps busy entrepreneurs, CEOs, and leaders write and publish a book to grow their business and become the authority in their field. Advantage authors comprise an exclusive community of industry professionals, idea-makers, and thought leaders. Do you have a book idea or manuscript for consideration? We would love to hear from you at **AdvantageMedia.com**.

In our first book, we dedicated our work to the people who mentored us, shaped our careers, and influenced our ideas around the changing workforce.

Our new dedication includes all those people but also includes all the other influencers we have been blessed to know and work with over the years, who really understood the work shift before everyone else. The people who recognized and championed a movement—long before the pandemic forced the world to recognize the benefits of a virtual workforce.

To all those people who came with us when the world was not ready for the change, you made it possible for The New World of Work *to arrive.*

CONTENTS

INTRODUCTION 1

SECTION 1
Where Did the Work Go?

CHAPTER 1 9
It's in Plain Sight, and It's Up to You to Find It

CHAPTER 2 21
Who Moved My Cube?

CHAPTER 3 33
Three Workforce Trends

CHAPTER 4 47
The Empowered Customer

SECTION 2
Work Fractionalized

CHAPTER 5 59
Tomorrow's Careers

CHAPTER 6 71
Capitalizing on Virtual Careers

CHAPTER 7 81
Rethink Your Career Strategy

CHAPTER 8 97
New Business Models for the Gig Economy

SECTION 3
Talent Globalized

CHAPTER 9 111
Competing for Virtual Talent

CHAPTER 10 119
Close the Talent Gap

CHAPTER 11 131
Motivating Tomorrow's Workforce

SECTION 4
Technology Virtualized

CHAPTER 12 149
The Customer Service Revolution

CHAPTER 13 159
Creating a Productive, Tech-Enabled Workforce

CHAPTER 14. 175
No Buildings, No Fear

CHAPTER 15. 185
Everything Is Digital

SECTION 5
Now What?

———

CHAPTER 16 193
Education Must Change (or Die)

CHAPTER 17. 201
Business and Purpose: Find Your Why

ABOUT THE AUTHORS 209

INTRODUCTION

When we were asked to create a second edition of *The New World of Work*, the realization set in that we had not only foreseen the radical change that virtual work offered but had actually *predicted* it over a decade ago.

There was significant evidence in the early 2000s that technology was driving the virtualization of work. There were also numerous clues that many workers preferred virtual and gig economy work.

History is replete with examples of economic transformations that, in retrospect, seemed perfectly logical. However, the human beings most directly affected by those changes did not *experience* them rationally. Instead, they experienced those economic course corrections as disconcerting and often terrifying. On the other hand, the people and companies that embraced these transformations often maximized new opportunities, revolutionized industries, and created generations of wealth—all because they could see the benefits of the change rather than the change itself.

As the authors of this book, our objective is to help professionals, corporations, and business owners negotiate this new world of work (NWoW). We are business leaders who have been successful in start-ups, small businesses, and large corporations.

As colleagues and friends for over two decades, we shared a range of market insights with each other about the monumental shifts in the way the world works. Although our early grasp of workforce changes was on target, it was after the pandemic that it became clear we had recognized a revolutionary market shift—before almost anyone understood its impact.

Ironically, decades ago, we both created companies leveraging next-generation work models, without realizing the magnitude of what was occurring. To us, it just felt like common sense. We became amused as we watched small and large corporations debate the value of virtual work.

We watched the gig economy expand leading up to the 2020 pandemic, which obviously disrupted the global workforce. The pandemic, although unfortunate for all who were affected by it, showed the world that virtual work was a necessity, as well as a better business model. Then the Great Resignation taught employers that workers would *not* return to the old, outdated workforce models. The talent marketplace we predicted was here to stay.

To be asked to catalogue our experience post-pandemic has been insightful. We are confident our perspectives and insights can educate both companies and professionals as they navigate the new world of work.

The virtual talent marketplace is here, and while it may be scary, this world is also exhilarating. Gig workers are now the workforce of the future. *Forbes* estimates as much as 40 percent of the US workforce is engaged in some type of gig work. This new gig economy offers those who choose to embrace it the opportunity to grow with *no boundaries.*

In creating this map to the new world, we have:

- provided a historical context to this new work perspective;

- outlined why we've reached the point of no return;

- demonstrated how to take advantage of this new marketplace; and

- introduced thought leaders who are capitalizing on the new world of work.

A very well-known example of someone with tremendous foresight, who took early action in this new world, is the visionary Pierre Omidyar, founder of eBay.

He was a real pioneer in the NWoW. You can imagine how shocked he must have been when, in 1995, a bidder paid $14.83 for a broken laser pointer on his new online auction site named after his consulting company, Echo Bay Technology Group.

When he personally contacted the winning bidder to reiterate that he was, in fact, buying a broken laser pointer, the first customer of eBay told the founder that he collected broken laser pointers and was very happy to have found another for his collection. This was the ultimate new-world expression of the old saying, "One man's trash is another man's treasure." And Omidyar was smart enough to realize that he could use technology to match people with their treasures—no matter how obscure or far away.

Thus began a revolutionary business that has grown to be an industry unto itself, with a base of fifty-five million buyers in all parts of the world. A more interesting fact, however, from the perspective of the new world of work, is that within a few years, eBay grew to over five hundred thousand sellers who considered eBay their primary source of income. If eBay employed all these people, it would be the second-largest retail employer in the world, right behind the behemoth named Walmart, founded by Sam Walton.

After eBay came Etsy, Upwork, FIVERR, ResultsResourcing, WeWork, Uber, DoorDash, Kaggle, and Freelancer—all fractional work platforms that don't care where you live as long as you're connected digitally.

> **Since the pandemic, it is impossible to find an organization that has not taken advantage of the free market gig economy, where people can monetize their skill set globally and sell their services to the highest bidder.**

Now, since the pandemic, it is impossible to find an organization that has not taken advantage of the free market gig economy, where people can monetize their skill set globally and sell their services to the highest bidder. The benefit is a two-way street; employers benefit as well because it provides the flexibility for seasonal and on-demand staffing requirements.

The most stunning statistic is that the gig workforce is on track to surpass the full-time workforce in size by 2027, according to a survey commissioned by Upwork and the Freelancers Union.

Strap on your seat belt, and let's explore this new frontier.

SECTION 1

Where Did the Work Go?

CHAPTER 1

It's in Plain Sight, and It's Up to You to Find It

There's a popular children's book called *Where's Waldo?* in which the lead character—with his signature red-and-white striped shirt and somewhat goofy expression—is obscured by various collections of people and things. He's hidden, but in plain sight (if you'll excuse the paradox), and it's the young reader's task to locate him in every illustration. By the end of the book, children become adept at locating the enigmatic Waldo in a glance.

We can only hope that this instructional parable reminds us of how the simplest truth can sometimes be obstructed by our need to make things complex. And so it is with the new world of work. If you want to know where the jobs are, here's a hint: They're in plain sight.

You might call this new, adult game "Where's the Work?" And the stakes couldn't be higher.

The Case of the Disappearing Jobs—or Not!

In listening to politicians and pundits, one might think jobs have been disrupted and workers have disappeared completely. They haven't! They're simply hiding in plain sight where only those who can see the obvious are able to find them.

For example, let's say a big company like IBM sets up operations in a new locale. In the past, the company would have staffed the new facility with a thousand new workers. That meant spending hundreds of thousands (maybe millions) of corporate dollars on office space, equipment, infrastructure, and parking lots. No more! Today the company rents space from WeWork (or any other flexible workspace) and staffs it with a few managers while the remaining positions are sent to the cloud to be filled by talent around the globe. Not because the labor is cheaper, but because the labor is more talented and more eager to compete for the work. That's right—*compete* for the work.

Work has spread across the globe because companies can now source talent easily, and the talent will compete for the work.

Why would a company such as IBM consider the cloud for its talent needs? Because technology and next-generation work now make it possible for companies to work effectively with skeleton crews on-site and large, competent resources spread across the globe.

And that brings us to an important point. You're right if you think much of the "new" work has gone overseas. Work has spread across the globe because companies can now source talent easily, and the talent will compete for the work, not based on price, but on the quality of their work.

Ironically, this doesn't mean those same jobs aren't also available in the United States—because they are. It's just that most Americans didn't realize that this work was available until the pandemic disrupted our lives. Many of them were not prepared to compete for work in this way.

Most US companies resisted virtual work models and struggled to capitalize on this budding talent war until they were forced to do so. You see, just as workers are competing for work in the cloud, companies must now compete for the best talent by providing interesting projects at competitive pay, regardless of what zip code the worker lives in.

Which is why we've created the second edition of this groundbreaking book. *The New World of Work* is both a road map for professionals seeking a career in this new world and a compass for those responsible for developing new virtual talent strategies around the globe.

The New Revolution

We're in the midst of a new work revolution, and its implications are as far-reaching as those of the Industrial Revolution, which lasted from 1750 to 1850 yet impacted the way we worked for generations after. The Industrial Revolution—coupled with the impact of the Great Depression—pushed jobs from the farm to the factory. The move from the farm to the factory, and then to the corporation, resulted in a geographical concentration of workers in cities and suburbs rather than dispersed on family farms. New industries evolved, in part to match the way our society worked, lived, and played. The *way* we worked after the Industrial Revolution ultimately reshaped our entire society.

There have been several mini revolutions since, but nothing to match the scale of the Industrial Revolution. That is, until now. The pandemic forced us to completely rethink work, technology, and the ways we connect.

NO BOUNDARIES: WORK DIDN'T DISAPPEAR—IT MOVED

The *Information* Revolution, which occurred over the last twenty years and has involved an almost unbelievable growth in work-enabling technology, has spawned an entirely new way of *organizing* work. This new method is responsible for innovative business models and career opportunities, all with one thing in common: Today, there are *no boundaries* to work.

> *Whether your workforce is onshore, offshore, near-shore, or virtual, the quality comes from the people, not the location.*
>
> —Tim McGrath, former senior vice president, customer service, Office Depot from 2000 to 2019; now founder of BAMG, which helps start-ups and small businesses establish world-class business operations

Over the last several decades, the world has experienced several well-publicized workforce developments. First, it was outsourcing, which led to offshoring. Today, there is a ubiquitous transformation of work platforms and talent sourcing that is revolutionizing not just how and where work is performed but the *way* business is being done.

This new form of work is leveraging the Information Revolution, and in the process transforming how and where we work. Today, work has clearly moved from the cube to the cloud, but in the process, it's created an entirely new breed of worker. More importantly, these models formed a talent *marketplace*.

THREE NEW-WORLD WORKFORCE TRENDS

This transformation, and thus the new work environment, has crystallized three trends that form the basis of this book. We will fully explore these trends and how you can leverage them throughout this book. The three trends are:

1. Work has been *fractionalized*. Routine work has been broken down into small tasks and, as a result, most companies do not need as many full-time workers because they outsource those routine tasks as contract projects.

2. Talent has been *globalized*. The fractionalization of work, combined with emerging technology, made talent truly exportable. Forget offshoring; the Gig Economy means that smart businesses can get talent anywhere, anytime. There are no more boundaries to work.

3. Technology has been *virtualized*. With work fractionalized and talent moving toward globalization, technology became completely virtualized *before* the pandemic. In fact, companies were able to move to virtual work models with more ease than even they imaged … when the pandemic *forced* them to do so. With cloud technology and its capacity to allow companies to leverage intellectual property, work (both contract and role-based) moved from the cube to the cloud. Professionals can work from anywhere and at any time, and they can even do so on their phone or laptop, at the beach, on a boat, or in their home.

In this new world, there are literally no limits to what, how, and where work can be performed. While this is clearly an advantage for those businesses that can adapt, it is an even bigger opportunity for professionals who learn how to compete effectively for this work. And, in a world with no boundaries, learning to compete for this work is paramount.

Throughout the book, we'll show you how to use these trends to position your business or career to compete effectively in a boundary-less world of work. Consider this your playbook for the game of your life.

> *Crowdsourcing and the new gig workforce are fascinating because they combine the natural tendency of humans to collaborate and break it into manageable, fractionalized work units. This model creates tremendous flexibility for both the worker and the employer.*
>
> —Roger Stiles, head of technology and global services, Fidelity Investments

Work, Work Everywhere ...

In "The Rime of the Ancient Mariner," the hero of the poem is dying of thirst while surrounded by an endless ocean of water. The now-famous line "Water, water everywhere, but nary a drop to drink" is all too appropriate for workers who struggle to take advantage of the new work that surrounds them.

According to the Gallup 2021 employment trends, 45 percent of full-time US employees worked from home either all (25 percent) or part of the time (20 percent).

Separately, Gallup's State of the Workforce study conducted with more than nine thousand American workers uncovered numerous reasons for employers to consider bringing remote workers back to the office in a hybrid fashion—spending part of the week at home and part on-site.

Most notably, the study revealed that:

- **Employees hope remote is here to stay.** Ninety-one percent of workers in the US working at least some of their hours remotely are hoping their ability to work at home persists after the pandemic.

- **Hybrid work is most preferred.** Overall, 54 percent of employees who work remotely at least some of the time say they would ideally like to split their time between working at home and in the office—a hybrid arrangement. A little over one-third (37 percent) would like to work from home exclusively, while 9 percent want to return to the office full time. Nearly half of fully on-site employees whose job can be done remotely wish they could work partially (37 percent) or exclusively (11 percent) from home.

- **Time preservation is a key reason for wanting to work remotely.** Not having to commute, needing flexibility to balance work and personal obligations, and improved well-being (which likely results from having more time) are the top-cited reasons for preferring remote work.

- **Employers are at risk of losing talent if they do not allow remote work.** Three in ten employees working remotely say they are extremely likely to seek another job if their company eliminates remote work.

- **Most workers don't foresee remote work harming company culture.** While most workers don't think remote work will improve their office culture, they don't think it will hurt it either. Two-thirds of all full-time US employees think that having people work remotely long term will have either no effect or a positive effect on their workplace culture; the remaining third think it will be negative.

- **Hybrid looks like the way of the remote future.** Seventy-six percent of remote workers say their employer will allow people to work remotely going forward, at least partially. Sixty-one percent of remote workers say they anticipate working hybrid for the next year and beyond, while 27 percent expect to be fully remote.

The other side of this coin is that, at the same time, businesses around the globe lament that they are unable to find qualified workers!

LinkedIn reports that the number of users changing jobs surged 50 percent from 2020 and nearly 30 percent from even pre-pandemic levels in 2019.[1]

At the same time, some workers hit pause or opted out completely. CNN found that 42 percent of working Americans surveyed considered taking a break from their career.[2] The Federal Reserve of St. Louis cited that three million Americans retired early because of COVID-19.[3]

---

1 Karin Kimbrough, "3 Reasons It's So Hard for Companies to Hire Right Now—and What They Can Do about It," CNN, November 2, 2021, https://www.cnn.com/2021/11/02/perspectives/linkedin-jobs-labor-shortage/index.html.

2 Ibid.

3 Miguel Faria-e-Castro, "The COVID Retirement Boom," Federal Reserve Bank of St. Louis, October 15, 2021, https://files.stlouisfed.org/files/htdocs/publications/economic-synopses/2021/10/15/the-covid-retirement-boom.pdf.

High quit rates are actually often the sign of a healthy and recovering labor market, where workers feel more confident in their prospects to go out and secure a better deal elsewhere.

What is unique is that most of those workers aren't just looking for a better job; they are looking for work that is flexible and work they enjoy. CNN and LinkedIn reported that the Great Resignation was more of a "Great Reshuffle" of talent and opportunity.[4]

This widespread career reshuffle could mean that workers will be more selective in their job search, holding out for the right opportunity versus jumping at the next best thing. Many are leaving for better compensation or more flexibility, while others are looking for something new and more fulfilling in their work. LinkedIn found that 73 percent of Americans said the pandemic changed the way they feel about their career and made them feel less fulfilled in their current jobs.[5]

While technology has enabled a new, virtual universe, the speed of business and technological change has outpaced the ability of many workers to adapt, resulting in a mismatch between work and the skill required to fulfill demand.

The jobs are there—in fact, businesses are crying out to fill them—workers just need to gain the necessary skills—and attitude—to make those jobs their own.

WE'LL BE YOUR GUIDES

For most, this alternate universe seemed to appear overnight. As two thought leaders who saw it early, at first even *we* didn't grasp the

---

4   Karin Kimbrough, "3 Reasons It's So Hard for Companies to Hire Right Now—and What They Can Do about It," CNN, November 2, 2021, https://www.cnn.com/2021/11/02/perspectives/linkedin-jobs-labor-shortage/index.html.

5   Ibid.

magnitude of the shift or understand the power of passion which fueled it. On behalf of those ready to embrace this fresh perspective, the new world will usher in new opportunities and shifts in the ways we approach business.

We know that such dramatic change can feel disconcerting. Understand that next-generation work is bigger than the cloud technology that enabled it. The gig economy is just that—a new *economy*.

> **Understand that next-generation work is bigger than the cloud technology that enabled it. The gig economy is just that—a new *economy*.**

You see, technology certainly has changed work. But it is a new breed of worker that is changing the way business is done. This new breed of worker competes for work anywhere in the world. They don't care if they are paid via a W-2 or a 1099, and benefits no longer drive their choices.

In 2013, Terri affectionately coined them "Virtualpreneurs"—combining an entrepreneurial spirit with virtual work platforms that match talent to the companies that want to hire them. These professionals don't care if they are paid via a W-2 or 1099; they have an entrepreneurial spirit and relish the freedom that virtual work offers.

That's why we had to release the second edition of this book. We felt compelled to explain this new world to the millions of companies that are still reeling from the Great Resignation, as well as the professionals who want to capitalize on the talent marketplace.

To grasp next-generation work, it is imperative to understand what—not *who*—moved the cube into the cloud. We'll show you why it's inaccurate (and unproductive) to blame the pandemic for disrupting the workforce.

Work had already shifted to the global marketplace years before the pandemic. Boundaries to talent had disintegrated and work was already moving fluidly around the globe, based on available and passionate talent. This is the effect of a ubiquitous trend that turned work into a marketplace rather than the result of COVID-19.

To truly understand this work ecosystem, let go of the need to blame and instead grasp that something much bigger is going on. Take advantage of the resources, set fear aside, and prepare for the future.

The fact that you've chosen to read this book is a very good indication that you are ready to get started. Companies that capitalize on these trends will have increased leverage through human capital. And professionals who create new career strategies geared to the new world will find their skills to be in high demand.

In the coming chapters, we will explore new businesses, careers and talent models driven by a cloud-based world and a workforce motivated by its *passion* for the work rather than the *location* of the job.

COVID-19 didn't disrupt the workforce. Passion did. The real benefit of removing the boundaries to work is that it enables one's passion for work to take precedence. And companies that can capitalize on passion will take a lead role in the coming Talent Revolution created by the NWoW.

If you're ready to capitalize on next-generation work and plot a new career strategy for yourself or a talent strategy for your business, then this movement is for you.

Welcome to a future powered by passion.

CHAPTER 2

Who Moved My Cube?

It may be terrifying for those caught in the vortex between the old and the new way of work. Most professionals earned the right degrees, responded to the demands of their professions, learned the intricacies of their industries, and were rewarded under the old system. It feels like a massive betrayal that this old system is falling away. Which is why it's a mistake to think that the Great Resignation was created by the pandemic.

The truth is that the cube was moved because passion is fueling a new breed of professionals. They are skilled and passionate global workers who want the freedom to choose the type of work rather than choosing a job based on its proximity to their homes.

Rather than being hindered by location, they are able to compete based on talent and passion. They skillfully leveraged cloud and mobile technologies and created the new world of work. And it was their

> **Companies that refuse to find virtual and hybrid work models will not thrive in this new marketplace.**

passion for work, rather than COVID-19, that caused work to seep across boundaries and find its way to this new marketplace.

Let this chapter be a call to action for those most affected by the new order. Professionals can reinvent themselves to compete in the new global marketplace. Conversely, companies that refuse to find virtual and hybrid work models will not thrive in this new marketplace. The best person for a job no longer lives within a fifty-mile radius of your corporation.

Where Have the Good Jobs Gone?

According to the International Monetary Fund, the global economy entered 2022 in a weaker position than previously expected.[6] Elevated inflation is expected to persist for longer than envisioned, with ongoing supply chain disruptions and workforce shortages impeding business recovery.

Every industrialized nation in the world is dealing with persistent, systemic talent shortages. This is chipping away at national resources, citizen satisfaction, and pure, old-fashioned hope, and it doesn't appear to be getting better.

The workforce gap is truly the most pressing issue in the industrialized world, but this challenge can easily be solved if companies and workers begin to think differently. *Talent is abundant, but the workforce is responding very differently than it did in the past.*

---

6   International Monetary Fund, "World Economic Outlook Update, January 2022: Rising Caseloads, a Disrupted Recovery, and Higher Inflation," January 2022, https://www.imf.org/en/Publications/WEO/Issues/2022/01/25/world-economic-outlook-update-january-2022.

FORGET THE CHEESE. WHO MOVED MY CUBE?

After the 2000–2001 dot-com bubble burst, an entertaining book helped displaced workers find their way through the aftermath of the Internet bust, and it became a catchphrase standard in common culture. The book was *Who Moved My Cheese?* by Spencer Johnson.

Unfortunately, this time it's not just the cheese that's moved, but also the restaurant, the farmers' market, and the grocery store. Everything is different. For the most part, business leaders can recognize that something about the talent marketplace appears to be different, but most executives can't put their fingers on what the problem is or where their darned cubes went. This is because they think this change is due to the pandemic rather than realizing it is simply a *better* way to work.

Here's why most leaders can't see the opportunities of next-generation work: They're looking for talent in old ways, which, in most cases, is no longer available.

IT'S TIME TO WAKE UP

Not only are workers not coming back the way corporations anticipated, but many aren't coming back in the traditional models we are familiar with. Work has been broken into small pieces and sent into the cloud for completion. The truth is that the talent isn't coming back, because everything we know about the talent marketplace tells us that work has been *fractionalized,* technology is now completely *virtualized,* and therefore talent is *globalized.*

Even traditional careers, such as professional sales positions, have been transformed. According to ZipRecruiter, sales roles increased by a staggering 65 percent in 2021.[7] More importantly, many of those

---

7   Patrick Thomas, "The Pay Is High and Jobs Are Plentiful, but Few Want to Go into Sales," *The Wall Street Journal*, July 14, 2021, https://www.wsj.com/articles/the-pay-is-high-and-jobs-are-plentiful-but-few-want-to-go-into-sales-11626255001.

roles take advantage of complimentary and tech-enabled channels, such as mobile sales tools and outsourced providers where contract labor is abundant.

Global professionals who want to compete in the new world of work must rethink their careers and begin the long road of rebranding and reinventing themselves. Like it or not, everything has changed.

The truth is, in the social/digital decade ahead of us (you know, the one where technology changes in an instant), jobs will change just as quickly. Professionals who want to thrive in this new environment have to think differently.

The online virtual-work market was valued at $1 billion in 2012. According to Emergen Research, the digital workplace market size was 19.6 billion in 2020.[8] That's a twenty-times increase in eight years. Another report said the digital workplace market is expected to grow to $72.2 billion by 2026, at a compound annual growth rate of 21.3 percent.

Take This Job and Move It

Let's explore a few roles that have changed in the last decade to help you better understand the cloud-based world around us.

Sales: Long before we imagined the new world of work, sales professionals were already working remotely to ensure they were in close proximity to their customers. Virtual offices (called "home offices") were common long before the tools to support it truly existed.

Administrative Assistants: Once a staple of corporate luxury, administrative assistant roles are almost all completely

---

8   Emergen Research, "Digital Workplace Industry Share, Growth: Digital Workplace Market Size and Forecast by 2028," April 2021, https://www.emergenresearch.com/industry-report/digital-workplace-market.

virtual. Today, these jobs are crowdsourced to hundreds of thousands of virtual assistants who now work from home. (Crowdsourcing is defined as a distributed problem-solving and production model.) Virtual assistants are finding their passion for getting things done combined with flexible schedules is a much better way to earn a living.

Accounting and Financial Analysts: Accountants and finance professionals are not usually known to adapt to new business models; however, virtual work models in this employment group were growing well before the pandemic. Companies like Tentho, and the two founders who combined forces to create it, quickly realized that the virtualization of technology meant that they, and their growing staff of accountants, bookkeepers, CFOs, and tax professionals, could work anywhere given the support of virtual tools.

Professionals: Professional jobs didn't go overseas this time. Instead, they went into the cloud and are picked up by professionals who choose to work from home. Today, there are over one hundred platforms where experts can take their knowledge to a virtual marketplace and sell it to the highest bidder. Whether it's ResultsResourcing, Chief of Stuff, Toptal, ListenersOnCall, or hundreds of other platforms, many professionals can find fractional work on job platforms rather than full-time roles. Moreover, there are now numerous training companies, such as Virtual Expert, that offer training to professionals looking to take their skills to market in this manner.

Engineers and Programmers: As technology has become streamlined, so have the ways in which it's programmed and engineered. Companies have moved this work into the cloud through platforms like Upwork, Freelancer, or TaskRabbit (as well as many others). That translates to a range of cloud-related development jobs—often from remote locations—for engineers and programmers.

Project Managers: Do you know that there are more contract jobs available to you on Upwork and ResultsResourcing than there are physical project management jobs available on recruiting job boards across the US?

Marketers: The gig economy has created multiple platforms *dedicated* to matching marketing talent with companies that need marketers. For passionate graphic designers, there's LogoTournament and 99designs, where designers compete openly and are paid based on the quality of work rather than the time spent doing it. Ten years ago, when we launched the first edition of *The New World of Work*, it seemed inconceivable that there would be multiple platforms dedicated to a marketplace just for marketing professionals.

The types of roles that are virtual are endless, which means it's time to think differently. The old workforce models disintegrated and were replaced by gig economy platforms that give professionals powerful new options for taking their passions and skills to market. Today, workers can create their own jobs. Workers can assemble work streams of projects that they enjoy rather than being forced to do tasks simply because they are considered part of a job description.

In this brave new world, the worker is in control of the jobs they select, the hours they work. Their choices are driven by their lifestyle and passion.

Platforms have transformed business opportunities for both sellers and buyers. In the virtual world that dominates large and small organizations, platforms are frequently where buyers and sellers meet, creating a global market for virtual services. Platforms are a valuable source of market intelligence, provide models for new practitioners in areas of expertise, and help solve the access to market and marketing requirements to fuel a business.

—Elizabeth Eiss, chief executive
officer of ResultsResourcing

EVEN THE HR DEPARTMENT CAN'T FIND THE CUBE

Just look at any job-posting board and observe a manic trend played out. Multiple companies with a significant amount of job openings, each with a variety of titles, and a usual mix of skills and experience required.

What's the deal? Are there really that many jobs? Are they the same jobs with different titles? Do they need people with such a wide range of skills? Recruiters inside and outside most companies are struggling to determine what talent is actually needed, yet everyone knows that they are short-staffed.

Workers are equally confused, and each job posting garners a ton of applicants, but the AI-powered job matching tools are struggling to have the job skills in the role description match up with qualified applicants. Why is this?

Yesterday's jobs don't exist, and tomorrow's career options are changing faster than a teenage girl changes clothes. As a result, most companies are caught between their old way of sourcing talent and these next-generation work models.

So both business leaders and working professionals are frantically looking for once-earthbound jobs. The fact that they can't see them doesn't mean they no longer exist; they have simply moved.

WORK MOVED INTO THE CLOUD

Here's how dramatically the job marketplace has changed: Currently, work opportunities are more readily available virtually than locally. And most of the new virtual work options are gig economy jobs with performance pay rather than the archaic and bureaucratic work system that compensated employees with wages and benefits for time well spent more so than work well done.

Since a large portion of the virtual work is being redistributed through contracts on virtual work platforms, those countries whose citizens access these platforms will win the jobs war, because that's where the work can be found.

The pandemic accelerated the need for virtual collaboration tools and mobile technology, which made it even easier for virtual work and created a hyper-available workforce digitally connected from anywhere and at any time.

For example, the Zoom video app was downloaded 485 million times in 2020, and 3.3 trillion meeting minutes are hosted on Zoom each year. That's an increase of 65 percent!

BEST COUNTRIES FOR GIG ECONOMY WORKERS

(Q2 2018-Q2 2019 EARNINGS INCREASE)

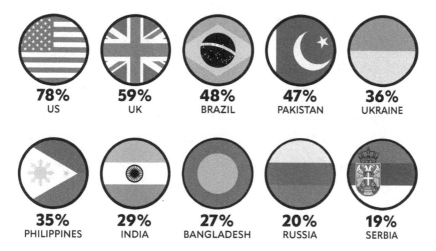

78%	59%	48%	47%	36%
US	UK	BRAZIL	PAKISTAN	UKRAINE

35%	29%	27%	20%	19%
PHILIPPINES	INDIA	BANGLADESH	RUSSIA	SERBIA

So, if the United States—*and its workers*—wants to win the job war, we must rethink the concept of work. Jobs have moved from the cube to the cloud, and the countries whose professionals capitalize on this trend will win the talent war.

You Can Win This War

For professionals who are left confused by the new talent market, the critical shift that must be made is to stop looking for jobs and to think more about work. You should be asking yourself:

- What type of work am I most passionate about?

- How do I prefer to work?

- What type of company and culture appeals to me?

- In what roles can I be effective?

Professionals who want to compete in this constantly changing environment have a huge advantage if they can build a new career strategy. *This book is designed to give professionals a map to this new world, whether that professional is a hiring manager, a corporate executive trying to develop a competitive talent strategy, or a job seeker stuck between worlds.*

> **Professionals who want to compete in this constantly changing environment have a huge advantage if they can build a new career strategy.**

Strengthened digital infrastructure now allows the world to work remotely, and monitoring tools provide more data and analytics to measure performance than any time in history. The Internet of Things and big data will continue to evolve so employers will be equally or more informed than if employees were sitting in a cube outside their door.

Without boundaries, workers are free to compete in new ways, and companies will compete for talent and maximize their future (and profits) one worker at a time.

So, what does tomorrow's workforce look like? What will be changed? What will remain the same? What are the trends, and how can we capitalize on them? We briefly introduced the three key trends in chapter 1, but let's take a closer look at them individually, learn what they mean for our economy, and find out why we should care. Understanding how these new trends have removed work boundaries is critical to maximizing the new world of work.

Let's explore these trends and begin to understand the road map to the new world of work.

CHAPTER 3

Three Workforce Trends

The transformation that created the gig economy wasn't COVID-19. The new world of work is driven by three key trends.

Work was *fractionalized* ...

Talent became *globalized* ...

Technology has been *virtualized* ...

Most professionals were forced to work virtually once the pandemic erupted our lives. However, the drivers of transformation were already reshaping the world of work. It just wasn't clear what the transformation was until COVID-19 jettisoned workers into the cloud. The future is here, whether we are ready or not.

Where Did the Work Go?

Back in 2009, a single question prompted us to research the talent marketplace, which ultimately led to the formation of this book: When the US economy lost eight million jobs, and the global economy lost millions more, *where did the work go?*

Not where did the people go, which is what the media and the government focus on, but where did the actual *work* go?

Even more curious, the majority of those "jobs" took on new forms as corporate profitability recovered and the gig economy took hold. So where did the actual work go?

Believe it or not, the work wasn't just outsourced or offshored. The gig economy is bigger than one country outsourcing jobs to another.

So, where is the actual work located today?

In order to answer the question of where the work went, we must first understand what happened to the *way* we work.

TREND 1: WORK IS NOW FRACTIONALIZED

Fractionalized work means that routine tasks (administration, project management, medical transcriptions, basic programming, and so on) have been broken down into small pieces and bundled together. That makes sense, but why do jobs look so different today? Why are there still high rates of jobs unfilled? It's not just because of the Great Resignation ...

The fundamentals of economic flow suggest that all markets will eventually find the most efficient path toward maximum utilization.

but rather the Great Reshuffling, as LinkedIn suggested.

The fundamentals of economic flow suggest that all markets will eventually find the most efficient path toward maximum utilization.

Companies are still looking for full-time workers to fill jobs rather than thinking about work in a more flexible way. For example, it would be more effective to find great managers who are well equipped to manage fractional work in a variety of models. Some work can be outsourced to contractors, some filled by virtual technology such as chat bots and artificial intelligence, and still other work performed by full-time staff.

Professionals should view work as a talent *marketplace* with more efficient ways to perform work than in the traditional job models of the past. Professionals who choose to embrace this new virtual career model will find plenty of work.

The fractionalization of work also enabled the next two trends to be realized.

TREND 2: TALENT HAS BEEN GLOBALIZED

Once work fractionalized, talent quickly became globalized, whether we like it or not. It is now more efficient to find talent globally than it is to search in the confines of a fifty-mile radius of the corporate headquarters.

Before the pandemic, you could look at any number of corporate headquarters of international companies. What was once a beehive of activity—floor after floor of project management teams, financial analysts, marketing teams, accounting teams, and all of the other professionals who are critical in getting the work completed—now sits empty.

At the same time, virtual offices, also known as coworking spaces, popped up all over the world, offering global memberships where workers could locate anywhere around the globe for a small monthly fee. The most notorious is WeWork, but there are hundreds of other options in every major city in the world.

This occurred pre-COVID-19. Today, more than 15 percent of all US office space is vacant, with some markets like Houston being as high as 23.5 percent. CBRE, a corporate office behemoth, estimates that coworking spaces will be 13 percent of all office space square footage by 2030.

Coworking space as share of total US office inventory

These spaces allow office renters to forgo traditional ten-year leases in exchange for shorter-term leases, from three to five years, or even on a montly basis. This type of flexible office space now makes up nearly two percent of all office space in the forty markets CBRE measures and is expected to grow to thirteen percent by 2030.

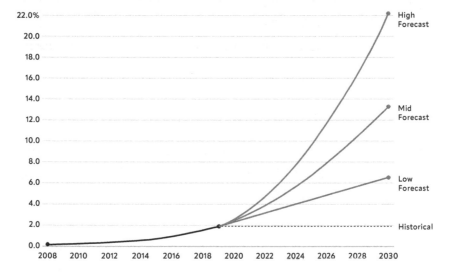

How did this happen?

Quite simply, the work *moved*.

When work moved from the farm to the factory in the early 1900s, it required centralized workforce models. Those companies that adopted new models gained a strategic advantage by leveraging the centralized workforce.

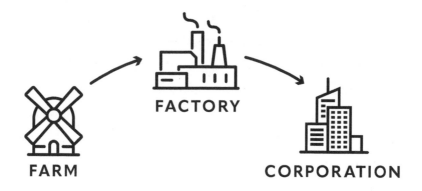

The reverse is true today: routine work is more effectively performed in a virtual, decentralized model. Because human capital has moved from the cube to the cloud, talent can be found virtually, regardless of country of origin. This isn't about jobs going overseas, it is about a new way of working that strikes at the heart of everything we once knew about work.

Smart companies can leverage the talent marketplace with literally no boundaries, and clever professionals can use the cloud to effortlessly take high-demand skills to this new market.

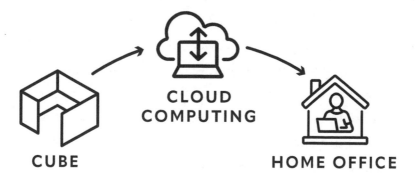

TREND 3: TECHNOLOGY HAS BEEN GLOBALIZED

What does it mean to virtualize work? Quite simply, it involves using new virtual technology to support a contingent, remote workforce. Many of the routine tasks that were performed in corporate cubes can now be performed virtually, from anyone's computer, and predominantly in home offices around the globe.

Quick, name one of the fastest-growing companies in the world. Google? Sure. Apple? Yes. What about Upwork?

Upwork Inc. (Nasdaq: UPWK) is the world's largest work marketplace. It connects businesses with independent talent. Upwork is the world's work marketplace, as measured by gross services volume. That amounted to Upwork's talent community earning over $3.3 billion on Upwork in 2021 across more than ten thousand skills in categories including website and app development, creative and design, customer support, finance and accounting, and operations.

Upwork serves everyone from one-person start-ups to over 30 percent of the Fortune 100 with a powerful, trust-driven platform that enables companies and talent to work together in new ways that unlock their potential. And they are not alone.

There are thousands of virtual work platforms, and they each retain 10–20 percent of the fees generated by matchmaking projects to talent, and they also supply both the bookkeeping and collaborative software, which both parties need to effectively communicate during the process. Demand for virtual workers is at an all-time high as corporations struggle to fill roles that were vacated during the pandemic.

The sheer flexibility that virtual work platforms offer companies is paramount. It allows companies to scale up or down based on seasonal or demand spikes, and it also allows work to be sent in the most efficient way for it to be delivered.

The fractionalization of work, making it easier to outsource, coupled with the virtualization of technology is good news for a company's bottom line as well.

According to Global Workplace Analytics, almost six out of ten employers identify cost savings as a major benefit of telecommuting. This includes costs such as:

- Rent and utilities

- Cleaning services

- Food

- Taxes

> *The trend toward the virtual workplace has changed everything—for businesses, workers, and landlords, who are renting much less space. Now businesses can save on things like brick-and-mortar costs and employee commutes. When you eliminate a commute, you save twenty to thirty minutes on each end of an employee's day, plus their transportation costs. It's like you gave them a raise and more free time.*
>
> —David Litman, chief executive officer,
> Travel Funders Network (David was also
> the founder and chief executive officer
> of Getaroom.com and Hotels.com.)

Everything is now digital, and businesses operate in a real-time environment, with limitless access to information and people. Companies can find better talent virtually, without borders, simultaneously increasing profitability, productivity, and worker satisfaction. *What business wouldn't sign up for that?*

However, for those organizations that fail to recognize the opportunities of virtualization, this is not good news.

Virtualization, like a wave crashing on the shore, picked up the work in its wake and dispersed it across the globe. Virtualization isn't just about the Internet; it's really the intersection of a range of enabling technologies and trends, and furthermore, it's a convergence of technology.

Convergence: A Technological Shift

To better grasp how these three trends affect our interactions in the workplace, let's look at some of the factors that drove change. The Information Revolution driven by technology was like an earthquake that began the shift to the new world of work. But the seismic shift that followed, and what is really powering this workforce transformation, is a technological shift known as convergence.

Convergence isn't about the Internet; the Internet boom in the late nineties wasn't the real innovation. It was the *access to information* the Internet enabled that spawned a new revolution and created the no-boundaries environment of the new world of work.

Rather than the Internet alone, it is the convergence of *more than one technology* that is enabling this new way of work. On many levels, it's historically similar to the convergence of steam technology and steel manufacturing, which propelled the Industrial Revolution and created the factory-centric model of work.

Without the simultaneous development in the iron and steel industries, advances in the early steam engines would not have been possible. As steam-powered rail transportation flourished, the transport of finished goods was more affordable.

Cheaper transportation resulted in more demand, thereby stimulating more expansion in factories and more use of iron and steel in the manufacturing of goods. That's how the convergence of the steel and steam industries became the linchpin for the Industrial Revolution, which powered the last radical workforce makeover, when work moved from the farm to the factory.

Today's technological convergence is more than transportation enablement. Convergence is based on transformational technologies *simultaneously* converging in the inflexible corporate structure. Each advance in technology enables faster and faster knowledge processing, creating global access to information at our fingertips. More importantly, every day these technologies simultaneously converge atop one another, exponentially multiplying to transform everything we do.

The core technologies that are converging in corporate infrastructure are:

- Cloud computing (software as a service and platform as a service)

- Social media

- Mobile and wearable technology

THE CONVERGENCE OF CLOUD COMPUTING, MOBILE, AND SOCIAL

SOCIAL AND MOBILE TECHNOLOGIES
BREED EXPONENTIAL POWER

The power of convergence isn't just these technologies operating independently; it's the simultaneous impact they are creating on the corporate and community structures. Let's look briefly at each, and then combine their effects.

Cloud computing is hot, but what's really heating up is the empowerment of small businesses and global Virtualpreneurs who no longer need expensive infrastructure to compete. Businesses can have world-class interaction and transaction infrastructure for a small fee per month, per license. A start-up can have a sales force automation system, a project management system, an accounting/finance suite, and a world-class customer relationship management system *combined* for less than $100 per month.

Why would any company not use the power of the cloud?

As cloud computing is making its way into our business tool kit, social media is changing the relationship between companies and its customers. Gone are the days when advertisements told us what to buy. Now our *friends* tell us what's in and which products and companies to avoid.

> *Young people coming into the workplace are all about working with new technology and social media. They're comfortable with devices and don't need human contact in the same way older generations did. What they do need is flexibility.*
>
> —Stephen Lynn, president and chief
> executive officer, Dovetail Software

More news is delivered through social media than on TV and radio combined. Virtual bloggers replaced broadcast news analysts, which is why that profession was also listed as one of the top ten dying professions in the "Disappearing Middle Class Jobs" article in *Forbes* magazine.[9]

Then, there's mobile and wearable tech. The power of this tool is not just the ability to talk on the phone but also the ability to *transact* on the phone. More transactions, from purchases on Amazon to orders for Domino's Pizza, are moving to mobile phones, without any human interaction to upsell or cross-sell. It's all done electronically. In 2010, it was rare to see someone authorize their credit card on a smartphone. Today, it is an everyday occurrence.

A good example of convergence is as close as your smartphone. Each day, millions of people around the globe—in highly industrialized areas and even third-world villages—use their mobile phones to *transact* business. This has created incredible opportunities for companies that have developed the infrastructure to capitalize on mobile transactions.

To put the new world in context, according to a study published by Mobile Payment Conference in 2018, the number of mobile-payment users in the US is expected to reach 74.9 million by 2022, in line with the growing use of mobile devices for paying taxes and other government bills.

Today, the growing accessibility of mobile commerce is wreaking havoc for governments accustomed to clear borders for e-commerce taxation and is quickly becoming the source of government scrutiny around the globe.

---

9   Jenna Goudreau, "In Pictures: 10 Disappearing Middle-Class Jobs," *Forbes*, June 23, 2011, https://www.forbes.com/2011/06/23/middle-class-jobs-disappearing-econ-omy_slide.html?sh=ff68c98554bb.

Mobile transactions are the epitome of the power of a convergence-driven marketplace that rips down borders and removes boundaries, irrespective of legislation or regulation. And, in this new world, finding talented people who can develop mobile commerce strategies is as easy as using Upwork. Go to the site, and up pops a list of virtual professional profiles with skills in the development of mobile commerce. It's that easy.

Convergence will continue to fuel the new world of work and widen the gap between those companies that embrace virtual work and those that don't.

Furthermore, the real power of convergence is the *simultaneous* impact of these technologies, which is reshaping the way we do business.

Organizations have now removed boundaries and broken down functional silos in a virtual environment so decisions can be made faster. As companies adopt the new model, there is a shift to speed within the organization since all teams now operate in real time in the stream. Leaders are more connected with teams, and output accelerates in a fast-paced environment. What used to take weeks and months now takes days and hours.

Convergence will continue to fuel the new world of work and widen the gap between those companies that embrace virtual work and those that don't.

Why You Should Care

Yes, the new world of work is here, and the boundaries have been ripped apart by a tidal wave known as convergence.

So, why should we care? Why should we pay attention?

Gig work will generate $455 billion in 2023, up 53 percent from 2020, according to a January 2021 Statista Research Department report.[10]

The companies that capitalize on these new trends will gain huge strategic talent advantages, cost, and expertise. And the professionals and employees of these companies will make themselves even more valuable and create totally new career models that we haven't even thought of yet.

For the corporation, the entrepreneur, the solopreneur, and the professional, there is one fundamental truth: Today's job will not exist in five years, and tomorrow's job hasn't been created yet. The only thing we have is the opportunity to capitalize on this dynamic and take no boundaries to the next level.

It is important to understand that the power of convergence isn't about big business, big government, or even the global talent marketplace. What is powering these workforce trends is the simultaneous *alignment* between the empowered workforce and the empowered customer. Both have whole new sets of tools and are ready to take control.

Tomorrow's workforce has indirectly partnered with today's customers and demands one thing: to be empowered.

---

10   "Gig Economy: Projected Gross Volume 2023," Statista.com (Statista, September 30, 2022), https://www.statista.com/statistics/1034564/gig-economy-projected-gross-volume/.

CHAPTER 4

The Empowered Customer

In addition to empowered workers, there is another *force* fueling the new world of work: the *empowered* customer. Customers today can create havoc on a company with a bad review, creating a social media war, setting up a hashtag that catches fire, or forming a virtual petition that spreads around the world.

Every business model since the birth of free enterprise has been centered on customers. If a new model were created to transform business, it would only work if customers also benefited. Truly disruptive business models are created when the customer becomes the catalyst for change. Just look at the recent advent of digital music or smartphone technology. Not only was the customer considered in R&D analyses, but in many cases, customers actually drove product innovation.

A perfect free market economy organizes what is produced or designed according to customer demand. The customer has and always will dictate what she wants and on what terms, and a business that understands what customers want will win the battle for their discretionary spend. Today's consumers are becoming more demanding and less loyal to traditional brands because they are empowered.

KPMG's survey of 18,520 consumers from more than twenty countries explores the truth about customer loyalty and how brands and retailers can attract and retain customer loyalty through enhancing customer loyalty programs.

Customer loyalty is certainly possible, but digital disruption and new generational influences show that the nature of loyalty is changing. Overall, only 37 percent of respondents identified reward points as one of the most effective ways to secure their brand loyalty, yet it is still one of the most widely used mechanisms of brand loyalty. Even more interesting, in almost every country, points and rewards were less likely to earn loyalty than corporate transparency and honesty.

When customers are loyal to a brand:

- 86 percent will recommend a company to friends and family.

- 66 percent are likely to write a positive online review after a good experience.

- 46 percent will remain loyal even after a bad experience.

Today, *as never before*, the customer has a new set of tools to communicate. With social media, customers can provide instant feedback on likes and dislikes, and do it in full, open view of the entire marketplace rather than behind a smoked glass window with researchers analyzing feedback.

Customer research is now as simple as reading Facebook, Twitter, Yelp, or Pinterest posts of any company brave enough to put a page into cyberspace. Whether making a Facebook post or setting up a boycott of a specific company's website, customers know they have the power to force companies to respond.

The tables have turned in this new world, and the customer clearly has control.

Perfecting Customer Service

As one of the best-known and successful online retailers, Amazon deals with literally thousands of customer service challenges every hour. While the volume of customer service queries is not that unusual for a company of this size, it is the way that Amazon deals with these queries that makes it stand out. The company states its philosophy simply: "Customer experience is more than customer service."

In a *Bloomberg Businessweek* article that dealt with Amazon's approach to customer service, it was noted that a customer had been "ripped off" on a purchase by someone selling his own goods through Amazon.[11] Rather than arguing about who was right and who was wrong, Amazon refunded all the money to the offended customer, even though she was not paying Amazon directly for purchased goods. The customer was quoted in the article as saying that she felt that Amazon was "standing up for her."

This story and others about Amazon's superior customer service have been spread rapidly through blogs, consumer websites, and traditional media such as *Businessweek*. As a result, positive digital word-

---

11　Christopher Coleman, "How to Create a Workplace People Never Want to Leave," Bloomberg, April 12, 2013, https://www.bloomberg.com/news/articles/2013-04-11/how-to-create-a-workplace-people-never-want-to-leave-by-googles-christopher-coleman#xj4y7vzkg?leadSource=uverify%20wall.

of-mouth feedback has rewarded Amazon with record-setting growth, while equally punishing other firms who were not customer centric.

Beyond Customer Service

With an empowered customer in a position of strength, companies are now viewing customer service as a primary differentiator. Labeled as "delivering a branded experience," businesses in every industry are stepping up efforts to provide superior customer service. And right on cue, the customer has become more demanding.

With an empowered customer in a position of strength, companies are now viewing customer service as a primary differentiator.

Now, the demands are quite interesting. These empowered customers don't just want great service; they want an integrated customer service *experience*, whether they call into a customer service center, send an email, make a Facebook post or tweet, or conduct an online chat session. Multichannel communication is now part of our daily lives, so the company that makes the customer's life easier, more convenient, and more organized through fully connected access to the company will win the hearts of the empowered customer.

Probably the best example of avant-garde customer experience is online shoe retailer, Zappos.com (Zappos). Asked frequently how they've grown so quickly, they note that the secret to their success is quite simple: "Customer service isn't a department, it's a way of doing business." The entire company is built *around* the customer.

Zappos offers free returns with a no-questions-asked policy. Okay, easy enough. Where's the revolution? Well, it's the little examples of extraordinarily great customer service that have become Zappos folklore.

- A Zappos employee sent flowers to a customer who ordered six different pairs of shoes because her feet were damaged by harsh medical treatments. The employee who sent the flowers felt like the customer needed something to lift her spirits.

- A customer service team member physically went to a rival shoe company to get a specific pair of shoes for a woman staying at the Mandalay Bay hotel in Las Vegas because Zappos ran out of stock.

- Zappos overnighted a free pair of shoes to the best man of a wedding party because he had forgotten to pack his shoes.

However, Zappos's website isn't drenched in self-praise. Instead, customer comments are clearly posted for the world to see. And the company posts all comments, not just the positive ones. Furthermore, good luck trying to find executive bios. The company's "Family" page is focused on department teams and how they serve rather than cold headshots of corporate executives who sit in an ivory tower and dictate the company's growth strategy.

Tony Hsieh, the late visionary and CEO of Zappos, detailed his legendary philosophy in his best-selling book, *Delivering Happiness*:

- Called "The Offer," Hsieh pays new hires $2,000 to quit if they're not happy at Zappos, figuring it costs more to employ unhappy employees.

- Build customer service into the entire company (rather than a separate department).

- Focus on company culture as the number-one priority.

- Apply research from the science of happiness to running a business.

- Help employees grow both personally and professionally.

- Seek to change the world and make money at the same time.

Consistently ranked among the top companies to work for in the world by *Fortune* magazine, Zappos was acquired by Amazon in 2009, and its sales continue to rise. All because they built their entire business model around the customer.

Technology Enabled the Customer

The coolest part of Zappos's customer-centric culture is the access it provides to any team member at any time through any channel. You can literally reach any department through a tweet, a Facebook comment, or the company's website, in addition to its call center.

Zappos *understands* these empowered new customers who demand 100 percent wired access, 100 percent of the time. This is the new requirement for their discretionary spend. No longer is this a nice-to-have differentiator. Total access has become what we like to call table stakes to the empowered customer.

Unlike many technological innovations of the past, the digital age has empowered the customer as fast as it has corporations and leagues of personnel. At home, consumers and businesses have access to social, mobile, video, and cloud services, including Facebook, Android, iPad, Foursquare, Google, YouTube, Office Online web apps, and Twitter; the list is endless and growing every day. Empowering technologies like these have never been made so readily available to users. This technology puts tremendous power directly into the hands of customers, who are happy to use it.

There is one constant with technology: *it changes all the time.* With this change, so goes customer demand. Customers have rapidly become accustomed to instant telephone and electronic communication and the ability to watch television programs on demand.

Artificial intelligence (AI) is also impacting the customer experience. Now machines can use big data to access customer preferences and predict customer issues and behavior. AI can assist the virtual workforce by guiding interactions and enabling knowledgeable workers to get their jobs done more efficiently.

One of our biggest fears is that AI and robotics will eliminate jobs, but futurist predictions are quite the opposite. AI will add jobs as AI models become more prevalent. Humans still have an advantage when it comes to emotional intelligence, ethical understanding, intent, and conversational design to enable AI to function. Job functions will change, but humans will be more valuable in the future.

Customers often have more information than a company's sales team or support staff. They can also wallop brands from their smartphone, with video even, while waiting impatiently in line for the company's employees to answer their questions. They can get recommendations from people in their business networks while listening to advertising or sales pitches. *Businesses must face the facts—the customer has control.*

Successful Employees Will Have Customer-Centric Tools

Over the past two decades, customers have obtained the means to find brands through search tools such as Google, Bing, and a large variety of others before the brands advertise them. These new tools make it easier for customers to reach out to their peers for feedback via social networks and word-of-mouth prior to spending one dime, regardless of any company-sponsored advertising.

Customers are empowered by information, connections, and feedback that they are using to drive purchase decisions. So, what does this have to do with the changes in the workplace? At the heart of the talent marketplace rests the empowered customer.

> **For businesses to serve an empowered customer, they must have capable employees who can directly engage the needs and expectations of empowered customers.**

Future job creation will differ dramatically from those in the past. Workers with strong communication, analytical, and problem-solving skills are in hot demand for one very important reason: for businesses to serve an empowered customer, they must have capable employees who can directly engage the needs and expectations of empowered customers.

And only *empowered employees* can solve the problems of empowered customers who now have a digital microphone that can reach across the globe. Employees who think critically and communicate effectively will be in demand for tomorrow's jobs.

The empowered customer has gained momentum over the last decade as social media launched them to even greater heights. Instantaneous, real-time feedback is available anywhere, anytime, on any product or service. Do you see the correlation to how people work anywhere, and at any time, on anything they desire? This similar, complementary overlay between the customer and the worker will create powerful opportunities for both segments while changing the way each interacts.

It is easier now than ever to express frustration or disappointment with a product or service. More importantly, it is easier than ever before to tell other consumers about your experience.

The same holds true for products or services that exceed one's expectations. Customer feedback has become the most trusted form of consumer-behavior influence. By tapping into this jet stream of positive exposure, a brand can reap the benefits of the empowered customer.

If empowered customers are driving the push toward the new world of work, the professionals who serve them are providing the fuel. Good jobs that are both personally fulfilling and critical to business success are waiting for those who understand the new dynamics of this environment.

In order to understand the new cloud-based work model, we must first dissect the fractionalization of work, understand the needs of the future workforce, and focus on the types of jobs best suited for virtualization and globalization.

In the next section, we'll look at how workers have changed and what really motivates this new virtual workforce. (Here's a hint: It's not about money anymore!)

SECTION 2

Work
Fractionalized

CHAPTER 5

Tomorrow's Careers

Chinese philosopher Confucius insightfully noted, "If you choose a job you love, you will never have to work a day in your life."

This belief is at the heart of professionals charting career paths in the new business environment. Their post-pandemic motto could be: "Do what you love, because nothing else matters."

Fractionalization has undoubtedly changed the world of work. Fractionalization is, in part, being driven by the changing motivations of workers who demand quality of life as part of their compensation mix. Ironically, for many workers, quality of life included flexible hours and work location *before* the pandemic.

What the pandemic exacerbated was the demand for meaningful work—which meant workers *everywhere* began to search for work they were passionate about. It's almost like the pandemic showed us that we could survive anything, and if life was going to be this tough, we might as well do what we love.

Of course, technology enablement had already reshaped the types of work that could be performed virtually. *The only difference now was that everyone could see it.* As more and more virtual work platforms emerge, and more and more gig workers join these ranks, the majority of traditional functions will ultimately move into the cloud. This has reshaped, and will continue to reshape, careers.

The real driver underpinning this change is *passion*. Workers are migrating to the types of work they *love* versus a job they are paid for (which frequently includes a lot of work they don't enjoy).

As a result of the massive distributional shift in the way we work, and the movement to work that is meaningful, career-planning strategies must be completely overhauled.

Forget asking your kids if they want to be doctors, lawyers, or teachers. That language will soon be obsolete, as more careers take on virtual characteristics and are ultimately reborn. The pandemic forced educators and students into virtual instruction, which forever reshaped the notion of what a teaching career looks like and created new education business models almost instantly.

And, with access to platforms such as LegalZoom.com and ZenBusiness, the majority of lower-level legal transactions can be performed virtually. What does that mean for paralegals and entry-level attorneys? It means a traditional job, in a traditional law office, is a thing of the past. As for physicians' careers, doctors are already able to perform a vast majority of diagnostic functions in the cloud. How will that change their career trajectory?

Tomorrow's career alternatives will become radically different over the next decade. In the old world of work, most professionals attended college and then chose a career. Although jobs may have changed over time, one's general career track usually stayed in the same hemisphere. An accountant typically stayed in accounting and engineers usually remained in R&D or operations. For the most part, we navigated within a general field of study from college through retirement.

Not anymore. Yesterday's jobs don't exist, today's jobs *won't exist* in a few years, and tomorrow's careers haven't even been created. Face it: We need a new methodology for career planning.

There's also something else affecting occupational strategies: Even the jobs that currently exist

> **Yesterday's jobs don't exist, today's jobs won't exist in a few years, and tomorrow's careers haven't even been created. Face it: We need a new methodology for career planning.**

within a corporation are becoming more difficult to categorize. For example, where will the social media department report to in the future? Should it be part of marketing or customer service? Or should social media be centralized in its own department? The same is true with customer service. Should customer service even be a department, or should it be embedded into every fiber of the corporate structure as Zappos did?

Corporate Walls Are Imploding

An interesting aspect of the new world of work and the virtualization of careers is that by taking away the boundaries of work, it indirectly affected corporate organizational structures. In company after company, the walls are imploding as the old way of organizing work collapses, without the boundaries that once held them firmly in place.

With convergence and the onslaught of cloud-based computing disintegrating the boundaries of work, career lines are simultaneously being blurred. Companies now need professionals that are *both* specialized and have a wide range of expertise. They need operationally minded marketers and sales-driven engineers. As the corporate walls implode, so do the boundaries of careers.

For example, one of the biggest battles being waged in today's corporations is the battle for the customer. In this social/digitally connected world, who handles social media–based customer service— the comments, interactions, and complaints?

Should it be handled by the customer service department? They used to take calls, but now their "conversations" are literally transparent on the social web. One bad service experience can be catapulted into cyberspace through Twitter and Facebook. Customer service has traditionally been managed by the operations function, yet suddenly marketing wants to control customer interactions to ensure a better brand experience. Marketers tend to be great communicators and can position things well, but they aren't used to working within the operationally centric customer service organization with its metrics and process efficiencies.

Public relations professionals should probably handle the issues that percolate through social media. They are certainly more adept at handling sensitive issues, but they, too, aren't used to speaking to an onslaught of customers.

The truth is, companies will not survive unless the hard-and-fast walls built around key functions start to come down, beginning with customer service. As a result of a convergence-driven need for truly cross-functional customer engagement, companies are struggling with finding the right talent to ensure their brands are received well in the transparent world of social media. Consequently, this is creating a revolutionary shift in hiring and outsourcing strategies, and it's happening at light speed. As a result, new workforce models and technology platforms are emerging overnight. And, because work no longer has to be performed *at* the corporation, companies are free to think differently about workforce solutions.

Better yet, professionals are able to think differently about their careers. The new environment is opening a new dialogue about the concept of a job, which will ultimately open the door to new career strategies. Just as in everything else in the new world of work, there will soon be no boundaries to careers, whether that career is inside the corporation or wrapped in the cloud.

New Thoughts on the Meaning of a Career

There are two forces reshaping tomorrow's careers—and they matter:

- **Gig economy careers:** As discussed, new crowdsourcing or virtual work platforms match professionals' passions for the types of work they *enjoy* with companies that wish to contract with them for various projects. This is rapidly shaping up to be one of the biggest income-replacement trends in the global economy. In 2012, Terri coined a new term for these workers: Virtualpreneurs. Many of these professionals are contract and 1099, but some corporations are finding they can leverage this type of gig worker in a W-2 model as well.

- **Legislative alignment:** The biggest barrier to growth in the new world of work in the US is legislation. The manner in which jobs are classified in some legislation, and the restrictions on the use of contractors versus employees, will not allow America to be competitive in the new world of work.

The gig economy, which now encompasses both freelance and W-2 workers, seeks to level that playing field. The gig economy created a new career altogether—the Virtualpreneur.

THE VIRTUALPRENEUR CAREER

Although projections differ, one thing is clear: the new world of work has ushered in a new career option—the Virtualpreneur. For professionals confident enough in their own ability, and desiring freedom and empowerment, almost any career today can be reinvented through the lens of a Virtualpreneur.

Although work-from-home positions have been growing since 2000, they were accelerating at rapid pace pre-pandemic. As of 2004, the US Bureau of Labor Statistics claimed that about twenty-one million workers, or 15 percent of the workforce, usually did some work at home as part of their primary job.[12] In 2011, that number had mushroomed to twenty-eight million, an increase of 12 percent from the previous five years.

Prior to the pandemic and Great Resignation, the number of self-employed people had increased at a dramatic rate. For example, in Intuit's September 2012 Small Business Employment Index, nearly 600,000 people went into business for themselves in the previous eleven months.[13] *That was ten years ago!*

This trend continued to rise, without many realizing it, throughout the last decade, emboldened with the advent of WeWork and other shared workspace options, which lease desk space to millions of gig workers around the world.

---

12   "Working at Home in 2004," US Bureau of Labor Statistics, September 23, 2005, https://www.bls.gov/opub/ted/2005/sept/wk3/art04.htm.

13   "Intuit Small Business Indexes Show Small Businesses Hurting," Intuit, September 5, 2012, https://s23.q4cdn.com/935127502/files/doc_news/archive/INTU_News_2012_9_5_General_Releases.pdf.

Virtual work, both freelance and W-2, which became known as the gig economy, was revolutionizing work well before the pandemic altered our lives. Today, according to the Gallup 2021 employment trends, 45 percent of full-time US employees worked from home either all (25 percent) or part of the time (20 percent).[14]

Gallup also found in its 2022 Future of Hybrid Work research that only 9 percent of workers with "remote-capable jobs" (now clearly obvious thanks to the pandemic) prefer returning to the office full time.[15] *Only 9 percent!* Like we said at the beginning, it's not who moved my cheese, but who moved the entire mall!

Put it all together and you have an unmistakable revolution underway. In fact, the number of work-from-home positions is expected to far outpace traditional employment job growth in the next five years.

The majority of these positions are in every type of work, even some deemed impossible to virtualize. COVID-19 assured that there would be significant deviations in home-based work models, facilitated by technological change, as empowered workers look for quality of life

> **This movement opened the door for an entirely new way of building your career, combining the benefit of virtual work with the continued expansion of available contract projects, as well as full-time roles, that the gig economy is bringing to market.**

---

14   Ben Wigert and Lydia Saad, "Remote Work Persisting and Trending Permanent," Gallup, September 2, 2022, https://news.gallup.com/poll/355907/remote-work-persisting-trending-permanent.aspx.

15   Ben Wigert, "The Future of Hybrid Work: 5 Key Questions Answered with Data," Gallup, March 15, 2022, https://www.gallup.com/workplace/390632/future-hybrid-work-key-questions-answered-data.aspx.

rather than long commutes and tiny cubes, as well as work they are passionate about.

This movement opened the door for an entirely new way of building your career, combining the benefit of virtual work with the continued expansion of available contract projects, as well as full-time roles, that the gig economy is bringing to market. We will explore a new career planning model in chapter 7.

The combination of technological change and workforce globalization is propelling firms toward a virtualization model. Add to this the need for flexible staffing models provide and presto, the Virtualpreneur was born.

Over a decade ago, Rand Corporation, a well-known think tank, called this a trend toward the "vertical disintegration of the firm." In other words, companies are shedding functions through outsourcing (and now crowdsourcing) in order to focus on specialized areas that define their core competencies. This is what we referred to earlier in the book as work fractionalization, or the breakup of traditional work roles into smaller, more specialized work units.

The forces driving the reorganization of work are simultaneously creating a shift toward nonstandard work arrangements such as self-employment and contract work. In this new work model, individuals compete in a global marketplace for project opportunities and work on multiple projects at a time. Teams continuously form, dissolve, and reform as old projects are completed and new projects begin. Some studies call this trend freelance, while others refer to it as micro-jobs. Because this new model combines freelancers and W-2 workers, the best description for it is the gig economy.

Regardless of the name, more positions are moving in this direction, and job placement site Indeed estimated there were about

9.8 million job vacancies as of July 2021.[16] In most cases, these positions don't require that workers be on-site, so they aren't tethered to the cube or required to work full time.

The challenge is that most companies aren't clear about where to find these workers, because they aren't being filled by the old job placement models of the past. The gig economy model could fill these positions *and* meet the needs of virtual professionals around the world.

A Virtualpreneur career is a viable option for professionals who want flexible work outside of a traditional office setting. No commute, nix the micromanaging boss, oust the nine-to-five workday, and schedule work around their lives rather than schedule their lives around the work.

The most important aspect of this trend toward the Virtualpreneur is that it allows people to do *what they love*! As previously noted, jobs of the past featured rewards that were driven only on a time-based, output-based system. The best part about this new career option is that it recognizes professional passions and rewards those who get results.

VIRTUALPRENEUR ACADEMY

The university system hasn't caught up to the new world of work, so Terri created Virtualpreneur Academy through Succeed On Purpose as a solution to the plaguing problem of ill-prepared professionals confused by the new world of work. Her vision was to tackle the problem of preparing workers to capitalize on this powerful career option. Virtualpreneur Academy includes five modules, each with a

---

16   Jed Kolko, "The Impact of Coronavirus on US Job Postings through July 16: Data from Indeed.com," Hiring Lab, July 21, 2021, https://www.hiringlab.org/2021/07/21/job-postings-through-july-16-2021/.

different focus, but all designed to teach professionals how to navigate the new world of work as Virtualpreneurs.

In 2012, this book *was* meant to be a wake-up call that there is a whole new way of working, and everything we knew about work is changing right before our eyes. Today, that is obvious. Yet, we want readers to understand that, while our economy was fighting through the pandemic and subsequent inflation-fueled recession, the boundaries to work disappeared *forever*.

> **Taking the best of entrepreneurial DNA and coupling it with the new virtual work models, the Virtualpreneur may be exactly what our country needs to regain its footing.**

This book is also about how we can compete as individuals and as a society and for jobs in the new world of work. It's also about how companies can compete by finding the most qualified people, regardless of where they live. And it's about how professionals can compete by opening themselves up to the new environment.

It starts with understanding that the hottest new career today is that of a Virtualpreneur. Taking the best of entrepreneurial DNA and coupling it with the new virtual work models, the Virtualpreneur may be exactly what our country needs to regain its footing and restore our fighting spirit.

In the next chapter, we'll explore how to capitalize on the new virtual career options and conquer this bold new world that Virtualpreneurs are taking by storm!

CHAPTER 6

Capitalizing on Virtual Careers

Buckle your seat belts, folks. Although you may not have heard about these professional options in the new world of work, they exist.

A Virtualpreneur career is a *real* opportunity for talented professionals to take their passion, as well as their skills, to the talent marketplace in a whole new way, be it freelance or full-time roles through companies such as Humach.

Many are finding this type of employment more satisfying, and in some cases, more lucrative. Although the person who chooses to be a Virtualpreneur must have the inner fortitude to deal with ambiguity, as well as the discipline to work with little or no supervision, if he or she chooses this path, the freedom is rewarding.

The gig economy created several business models that are proven to take professional skills to market virtually, from recruiters who now match companies with full-time staff or virtual freelancers.

Others use a crowdsourcing model to drive success and operate like a virtual work matchmaking platform. These new virtual work platforms are revolutionizing the way work is done. They have eliminated the boundaries of work and actively bring customers who want to hire talent to their platform proactively.

Virtual work platforms are basically virtual employment offices that offer projects professionals can pick up and put down as needed. In some cases, workers bid on jobs posted by hiring companies, or they can post their own advertisement.

> **This whole new way of working means that rather than having a single job with one company, you can have a variety of roles, doing work you love, for a lot of different companies.**

Virtual work platforms use *work bidding* to match contract jobs with contract workers. This model is proving to be very effective. Let's look at how some companies are driving the evolution of this new job-matching approach.

What's powering this new way of working is work being fractionalized. Once full-time positions have been broken into smaller job units (fractionalized) that can now be offered to gig workers.

This whole new way of working means that rather than having a single job with one company, you can have a variety of roles, doing work you love, for a lot of different companies. It's almost like spreading your eggs across multiple baskets rather than putting them all in one.

Change Your Perspective

There is one barrier that will keep many US professionals from pursuing a Virtualpreneur career. It is the access to traditional workplace benefits such as health insurance, life insurance, disability insurance, and paid education or training.

In a traditional employer/employee relationship, workers expect these benefits as part of their compensation. The challenge is that these benefits have created a *dependency* on standard corporate work arrangements, and most US workers consequently ignore contract work because of the absence of health insurance. This is a mistake for several reasons.

In 2014, the full force of the Affordable Care Act (ACA) changed this landscape completely. The Affordable Care Act (ACA) is a comprehensive reform law; it increased health insurance coverage for the uninsured and implemented reforms to the health insurance market. This included many provisions that are consistent with AMA policy and holds the potential for a better healthcare system, making health insurance benefits available to those not covered by corporate plans.

By 2016, the uninsured share of the population had roughly halved, with estimates ranging from 20 to 24 million additional people covered. The law also enacted a host of delivery system reforms intended to constrain healthcare costs and improve quality. After it went into effect, increases in overall healthcare spending slowed, including premiums for employer-based insurance plans.

Many, if not most, traditional companies stopped offering any type of insurance benefits due to skyrocketing costs and the availability of the ACA. Although the law continues to be politically divisive, the pandemic may have sealed its fate.

Whatever happens in the ongoing political wrangling about affordable healthcare, the fact remains the same: these benefits will never be the same as they were twenty years ago. Companies can't afford to offer them either. Therefore, the argument that a professional should take a traditional job for its benefits is flawed.

THE FIRST VIRTUAL EXPERT

When Kathy Goughenour walked out of her Fortune 500 corporate career in 2001, she didn't even know what a virtual "expert" was. At the time, her boss told her she would never make her same salary elsewhere and that she should be grateful for what this position offered. It was the kind of jolt that she needed to take the leap, and Kathy promised herself she would double her salary. Within her first three years, she created a six-figure business and loved the freedom to do the work she enjoyed, as well as work from wherever she wanted. Others started asking her for advice, and she soon began training other professionals looking to make the leap. She went on to trademark the idea of a Virtual Expert and created a million-dollar training enterprise serving virtual assistants and Virtual Experts as they transitioned to virtual work.

> *Since starting my own virtual business in 2001, I watched the virtual industry grow both in client demand and in the desired traits of freelancers. Demand increased first because business owners saw the value of hiring independent contractors who could work on an as-needed basis, saving employee overhead costs.*

Demand grew even faster after the pandemic hit, and all executives and business owners, whether virtual or not, were forced to work virtually and needed both employees and freelancers.

Business leaders quickly discovered the benefits of both working virtually as well as working with independent contractors. Traits desired by hiring managers shifted when they realized how efficient and effective it was to hire experts rather than generalists.

In researching the top traits required for virtual professionals, I discovered that managers and business owners alike were willing to pay a premium for experts who had problem-solving skills and were proactive professionals. That's when I came up with and then trademarked the name Virtual Expert.

—Kathy Goughenour, chief executive officer and founder of Virtual Expert

How to Succeed as a Virtualpreneur

Success means different things to different people. For Virtualpreneurs, success typically means earning a competitive wage for work they enjoy and the freedom to do that work when, and from where, they choose.

Success as a Virtualpreneur requires several attributes. However, the most accurate predictor of success as a Virtualpreneur is the ability to shift one's mindset about work. This means letting go of the attachment to a set monthly income and corporate benefits. The focus becomes on work performed and the value of that work.

Prior to the pandemic, many perceived this as a lack of security, when in reality, it is as secure as the old way of work. Being a Virtualpreneur is a viable career option for professionals who want more control over their careers and desire more flexibility. It's also quickly becoming a powerful trend for companies to mitigate high overhead and rapidly changing workforce needs.

There are numerous careers that can easily be ported to a Virtualpreneur career model, and we expect that this list will continue to grow. They include:

- **Customer service agents:** The backbone of the work-at-home sector is customer service agents, a job that is attractive to both younger and older workers.

- **Virtual assistants**: The once-lucrative field of the administrative assistant has now been either eliminated or replaced by virtual assistants.

- **Writers:** Jobs for writers and editors are in abundance across the web. From newspaper blogging to book editing, there is no shortage of positions for effective writers looking to earn income.

- **Teaching:** More and more classes are being offered online, and this trend is expected to increase.

- **Mystery shoppers:** More than just liking a store, mystery shoppers evaluate an end-to-end brand experience from a customer perspective.

- **Problem solvers:** Businesses have a glut of problems and are frequently looking for professionals skilled at problem identification and resolution.

- **Project managers:** Always an important skill, virtual project managers are in hot demand globally.

- **IT professionals:** Several virtual work platforms cater only to IT professionals and include traditional programming as well as new programming languages to capitalize on the mobile application boom.

HOW TO MAKE A VIRTUALPRENEUR CAREER SUCCESSFUL

As more and more professions take on virtual characteristics, this career option will become a sought-after choice for workers in the US, as well as around the globe. Although being a Virtualpreneur is not for everyone, most professionals who are attracted to this model as a career option have the basic attributes that would ensure their success. There are four key traits that are necessary to make a Virtualpreneur career successful. These include:

1. **Self-motivation:** Virtualpreneurs don't have bosses telling them what, where, and how to perform work. The more self-motivated the Virtualpreneur, the more successful he or she will be.

2. **Prioritization skills:** Since there will be multiple projects with a variety of deadlines, Virtualpreneurs must be able to self-prioritize projects and manage client expectations.

3. **Resourcefulness:** Without the attachment to the corporate machine, resourcefulness is critical. Virtualpreneurs creatively

use their social and technical skills to find tools, additional projects, and unique solutions to work problems. Trial and error is part of the equation, and Virtualpreneurs tend to be creative problem solvers.

4. **Basic technical skills:** Virtualpreneurs must be virtually connected and capable of managing their own personal computer and network connections. The good news is that there are virtual tools to assist in this task, which most workers picked up easily during the pandemic.

So, for professionals who want to capitalize on the new world of work, the message is simple: give up the cube and the commute and look to the cloud. That's where the work and opportunities are. To capitalize on the new world of work, follow your passions and think outside the box. Remember, there are no boundaries.

Finally, let's look at some compelling reasons to consider this career:

- **Access:** For starters, it's the most lucrative career option available to most professionals. Although, like any contract-based positions, it takes time to build up a base of clients, the virtual work platforms make it much easier to find work than in other entrepreneurial endeavors. There are reasons for the success of Upwork and ResultsResourcing—there is work! It's just no longer in the cube and has moved into the cloud, and the *home* is now the office of tomorrow.

- **Work:** PayScale surveyed over 682 employers for insights into how organizations are changing their approach to remote work after the COVID-19 pandemic. Seventy-three percent of organizations believe that remote work will change the competitive talent landscape, and 50 percent said they will have a flexible or hybrid office after the pandemic.

- **Market:** More and more companies are looking to virtual workers to fill roles, especially during times of change and transition, which will likely continue as the aftereffects of the pandemic continue to work their way through the global economy.

Now that you know the work is out there for you, you no longer need to fear the journey beyond the four walls of the corporation. Take your skills to the virtual work marketplace.

A "marketplace" is a location where supply (workers) meets demand (job roles). The good news for everyone is that the new world of work created a talent marketplace that you can capitalize on.

To do so … you just need a new career strategy.

CHAPTER 7

Rethink Your Career Strategy

When the first edition of *The New World of Work* was released ten years ago, we knew that the boundaries to work were disintegrating quickly. We also recognized that with the fractionalization of work taking hold, workers could compete for gig economy jobs from anywhere in the world.

We also predicted that these trends would create a global *marketplace* where workers and companies that needed each other found each other in the cloud. This marketplace became known as the gig economy.

Let's start by looking at the gig economy from workers' perspectives, and then we'll shine a light on how companies can compete for global talent in this virtual marketplace.

Carl Pascale spent twenty-two lucrative years with Lockheed Martin before being jettisoned in one of several corporate layoff rounds. Carl thought finding another job would be easy. However, after nearly ten months of searching and countless workshops and seminars from so-called experts, Carl had nothing. He was bewildered.

In the summer of 2012, he asked a question that struck fear in his heart: "How can so many people be following such good advice on their job search and not getting results? Is it possible that these experts could be wrong, and that maybe the career marketplace has changed?" The question changed his entire focus. Shortly after his fated self-imposed question, Carl heard Terri Maxwell speak on the talent market shift (the basis for parts of this book) and started the process of waking up.

"The old way isn't working. There are talented professionals in the marketplace, but they can't seem to find any open doors because they are looking for the jobs that they lost. But they no longer exist! Now that I understand the new world of work, I'm not going back. I don't know where this road will lead, but I know that I want to be part of building something that makes a difference. My advice to those on this search is that you have to let go of what you knew about the talent marketplace to find open doors."

—Carl Pascale

For professionals navigating the new world of work, the journey can seem overwhelming and frightening. Although it's certainly a different frontier, moving from the cube to the cloud should not be frightening. The new world of work is ripe with opportunity for professionals who understand how to map new career strategies.

A Quick Review

Let's recap a few critical points from previous chapters.

First, the new world of work is based on three revolutionary workforce trends:

1. **Work has been fractionalized.** Routine work has been broken down into small tasks and, as a result, most companies do not need as many full-time workers because they outsource those routine tasks as contract projects.

2. **Talent has been globalized.** The fractionalization of work, combined with emerging technology, made talent truly exportable. Forget offshoring; the gig economy means that smart businesses can get talent anywhere, anytime. There are no more boundaries to work.

3. **Technology has been virtualized.** With work fractionalized and talent moving toward globalization, technology became completely virtualized *before* the pandemic. In fact, companies were able to move to virtual work models with more ease than even they imaged … when the pandemic *forced* them to do so. With cloud technology and its capacity to allow companies to leverage intellectual property, work (both contract and role-based) moved from the cube to the cloud. Professionals can work from anywhere and at any time, and they can even do so

on their phone or laptop, at the beach, on a boat, or in their home. (We'll cover this in more detail in section 4.)

These trends mean that jobs as we know them have changed. Today, work opportunities are everywhere (because they are global), and this chapter will give readers a map to find Waldo in this new world of work. The majority of work opportunities exist in two segments:

1. **Virtualpreneur career options:** There are numerous work opportunities for virtual professionals who want to take their talents to market through a virtual work platform, or through companies like Humach. These models, as we explored in the last chapter, are the basis of the gig economy that was thriving pre-pandemic and is now an indelible part of the future of work.

2. **Roles in small businesses (under $100 million in revenue):** The majority of positions, both full time and contract, reside in small businesses, not large corporations. Most displaced workers were catapulted from large and small corporations alike during the pandemic. However, the majority of the job growth today is within small companies with revenues under $100 million. The challenge for most professionals is that small companies don't hire the same way large corporations do, and workers don't know how to find this readily available employment. Small businesses rarely advertise open positions, but instead prefer to fill them through referrals, networking or through a virtual work platform. In many cases, small businesses are looking for professionals to fill roles rather than workers to fill jobs, which means typical job postings are irrelevant or nonexistent in most small businesses.

Finding Your Place in the New World of Work

Whether you're looking to become a Virtualpreneur or looking for a job that offers virtual work, one thing is true: you need an entirely new career strategy. Gone are the days where professionals earn a degree in one field, join a company, and work up the corporate ladder in that same profession. Today, gig workers compete globally and work their way up their own personal ladder of success.

Making the Leap to a Virtualpreneur Career Strategy

For anyone seeking a career change, hopefully this book has encouraged you to think about becoming a Virtualpreneur. For all the reasons noted in the last section, not to mention the impact of the pandemic, it is by far the hottest career trend of this next decade. A secure, standard-paying job is an illusion in the post-pandemic economy, and a traditional employment relationship now offers only a pittance of economic security. Yet opportunities abound in the gig economy.

The biggest leap professionals must make is to give up dependence on traditional benefits. Prior to the pandemic, the hard part of entering the gig economy was giving up the perceived reliance on once-secure corporate benefits. The pandemic made this choice obvious, and most workers feel more secure in the gig economy, which offers the benefit of flexible schedules, as well as work they are more passionate about.

The interesting thing about the gig economy is the actual structure of work. In more traditional job functions, work is structured and ordered, managed, and managed again. There are opportunities for career progression and regular oversight from managers.

Conversely, gig workers choose the types of work they enjoy, are paid for the output they deliver (versus the time they sit in a cubicle), and have the freedom to work from wherever they want. In the Virtualpreneur world, the individual is responsible for seeking projects capitalizing on the demand for their services.

There is no well-defined career ladder, yet the rewards of freedom and the ability to increase earnings based on performance far outweigh the limitations of this new system. A Virtualpreneur career is a great option for those who want structured work opportunities without the micromanagement of a corporation.

What are the three best reasons to give up the search for a job and seek a Virtualpreneur option? They are *opportunity*, *passion*, and *freedom*.

So, would you make a good Virtualpreneur, or are your skills better suited for a full-time role in a small business? Succeed On Purpose created a powerful tool to help professionals develop a career strategy for the global talent marketplace.

Building a Career Strategy

The move toward working in the gig economy ushered in a new way to think about career planning. Another factor driving career change is that most work opportunities are being created by small businesses rather than large corporations. In the social/digital decade ahead of us, where technology changes in an instant, so too will the jobs. In addition, the vast number of jobs available in the next decade will be in smaller businesses, and their methods of hiring are not the same as large corporations.

Instead of worrying about your job, build a new *career framework* and operate within it. After working with professionals in varying stages of career transition, Succeed On Purpose created a career-planning system to prepare professionals for this new world of work. This system has been used by thousands of professionals and Virtualpreneurs through the Get Clarity program Succeed On Purpose offers.

The Succeed On Purpose Career Planner serves as a map to this new world and uses a series of decisions for career planning. It starts with three simple personas. (Personas are like identities.)

BUILDER
Motivated by **building** things (ideas, programs) and creating value.

SOLVER
Motivated by **solving** problems and experiencing freedom.

DOER
Motivated by **doing tasks** and operating in a familiar structure.

Image courtesy of Succeed On Purpose

Decision 1: Your career strategy starts with career personas. Are you a doer, solver, or builder? (See the image above). We've outlined descriptions of each of the personas to assist you in this process. The material should also help business owners and talent executives find people with the right qualifications for given projects or positions.

The doer: A *doer* persona prefers a familiar environment and a predictable set of responsibilities. Although tasks might change, *doers* function best in a familiar structure. They are motivated by getting things done and by operating in the "known." They prefer structured work and the opportunity to get things done. *Doers* tend to navigate to more routine functions: administration, operations, accounting, and IT.

If you have a *doer* persona, your career choices should focus on roles in corporations or small businesses where duties are somewhat predictable. If you elect a Virtualpreneur path, look for stable contracts with well-known virtual work platforms, like those outlined in this book. Business owners and hiring executives should remember that *doers* prefer predictable work and are easily empowered by intrinsic self-motivation. Therefore, they make perfect additions to any team, project, or company.

The solver: A *solver* persona is highly motivated to solve problems. *Solver* personas have a wide range of career choices in this new virtualized world. Whether they lead a team, work on a team, or work alone is irrelevant. Business owners and executives will find that they have a burning desire to solve problems and work best when given the freedom to do so.

Because most corporations typically "outsource" problem-solving assignments to boutique consulting firms or through gig economy workers, those *solver* professionals can easily replace their incomes doing contract consulting, virtually and locally. In fact, *solvers* make great solopreneurs and Virtualpreneurs, whether they are 1099 or W-2.

Conversely, *solvers* are also in demand in most companies that need analytical problem solvers to address myriad challenges. Either way, *solvers* have a variety of career options available to them, if they follow their core nature: solving.

The builder: The *builder* persona is a powerful force in smaller businesses, under $100 million in revenue, as well as start-ups. *Builders* are never satisfied with the status quo; they *must* build something. And once it's built, they need to make it bigger or better, or move on to the next thing.

Builders are tapped for difficult projects: building new departments, creating new methodologies, or carving out new territories. They show up in every discipline and can be uniquely identified by their drive to build something of value. They will change jobs every one to three years, even if it's with the same company.

Business owners and managers know that *builders* make great entrepreneurs and powerful leaders in companies of all sizes. However, they do not perform well in hierarchical corporate structures. *Builders* excel in small businesses that are growth oriented. *Builders* invent, create, build, solve, and serve in a variety of roles across all industries.

The key for a *builder* persona isn't what they do, but *how* they do it. They must feel as if they are building something of value.

SUCCEED ON PURPOSE CAREER PLANNER

Decision 1

BUSINESS/CAREER PERSONA

Image courtesy of Succeed On Purpose

As you reflect on your career, don't think about traditional career tracks. Think about your persona. Which persona best describes you? Focus on the framework and target your job, career, or business search using this framework. Once you've decided on your persona, advance to the second decision: How would you prefer to work?

Decision 2

PERSONA-BASED WORK OPTIONS

Image courtesy of Succeed On Purpose

Evaluate your persona-based work options. Does your persona fit a role working in a larger corporation (above $100 million in revenue) or a small business (under $100 million in revenue) or possibly a start-up, or should you evaluate virtual work platforms, or start a business or franchise? (See Decision 2.)

Decision 3

Based on whether or not your career persona is better suited for that of an entrepreneur or a role working for someone else, evaluate the categories of careers available to you.

Should you consider becoming a Virtualpreneur and making your way on a virtual work platform such as ResultsResourcing, Upwork, or Toptal? Should you try to build a solopreneur business as a consultant, coach, trainer, etc.? There are many local solopreneur opportunities. Or should you start a business franchise, become an entrepreneur, or build a business based on something you enjoy?

If you're better suited for working for someone, find companies that are capitalizing on the gig economy, like Humach. You can have the benefits of full- or part-time W-2 work, yet work remotely and on a flexible work schedule.

If you're better suited for working inside a company, another consideration is the size of business. Each business segment has a need for something different based on its evolutionary state, which we'll explore later in this chapter.

New World of Work: Career Planning Strategy

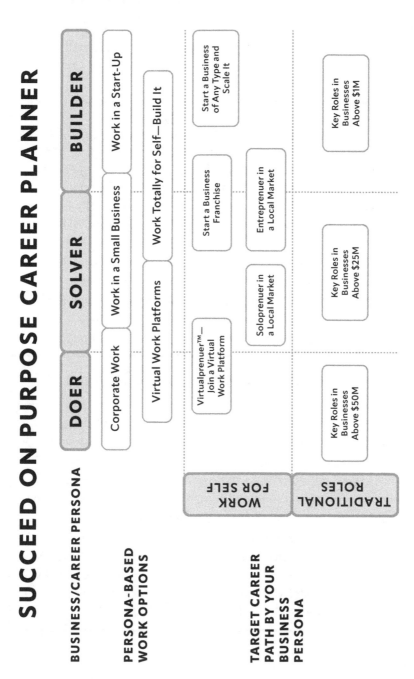

Image courtesy of Succeed on Purpose

As part of your career strategy, knowing the size of the companies you want to work with (whether doing contract or role-based work) is critical. Companies take on different personalities based on their revenue size. Succeed On Purpose has prepared this chart to assist professionals in identifying the characteristics of a specific small business segment.

MICRO BUSINESS OR START-UP: **UNDER $1 MILLION IN REVENUE**
Much like an infant, start-ups are messy, and they change almost daily. They need a lot of care and feeding, and usually only builders are suited for a start-up environment, and all the builder roles (change agent, team builder, execution driver, and game changer) are sought out by start-up executives looking to build their management teams. Risk is high and pay is usually low; however, there are tremendous rewards for those professionals who find a great start-up and stick out the ups and downs. Professionals who seek these opportunities must enjoy hard, creative work and enjoy a business environment that changes constantly.
SMALL BUSINESS: $1–$10 MILLION IN REVENUE
Small businesses that have survived "the first million" and are up and running move on to this next stage. Small businesses are a little more structured than start-ups, but still change very rapidly, in part dependent upon how fast they are growing. They can be thought of as young children. A business of this size is still changing, growing, and learning new things but is no longer as messy as the infant. Small businesses have typically found strategies to consistently grow revenue and have the basic operational infrastructure underway. The key in this phase is scale. Can they scale what they built? They tend to seek connectors, execution drivers, task masters, and problem solvers.

MEDIUM BUSINESS: $10–$50 MILLION IN REVENUE

This is a very fun business stage. Medium businesses are like middle-school children: they are maturing and are finding their rebellious voices. They tend to be a little arrogant, in part because they made it through the previous two phases (start-up and small business) and have experienced some success. Many businesses get stuck in this stage, in part because what got them to this phase is *not* what will get them to the next level. Smart businesses bring on experienced management teams at this phase, and the owners move into leadership roles. Those business owners who continue to try to manage the day-to-day activities of a company in this segment size tend to get stuck here and never realize their potential. There are *many* opportunities in companies of this size. Selecting a company with the best cultural fit and one in which there is a competent management team is paramount. Also, companies of this size usually seek outside investors, which changes their culture and growth trajectory. Businesses of this size create lots of professional opportunity and tend to look for the following roles: team builders, strategists, problem solvers, task masters, game changers, and execution drivers.

LARGE BUSINESS: $50–$100 MILLION IN REVENUE

This is a very interesting business stage. The business has shed its puberty-like rebellion and has settled into its destiny, strategy, and plan. It has usually found a competent management team to support the business founder(s) and usually is well positioned for scalability, if well-funded. There are two critical components that determine how a company performs in this stage: its ability to build a collaborative team and its ability to execute its strategy. Typically, the company takes on an alter ego and either sees itself as a billion-dollar business, and consequently starts to act like one, or it prefers its small-business roots and tends to cycle its strategies, without growing at the same trajectory. It's paramount that professionals understand which of those personas the small business has taken on, as they behave very differently. A company that sees its identity as that of a billion-dollar business tends to be more collaborative, and less political. A company that identifies with its small-business roots tends to become mired in political battles and unfortunately rewards loyalty over performance. All roles are equally sought after, and job security is much more stable, as long as the company continues to grow.

If you're not sure whether you should head down the path to being a Virtualpreneur, solopreneur, entrepreneur, or a full-time role, Succeed On Purpose offers an affordable and powerful program, Get Clarity, to walk professionals through the four steps of meaningful work: persona, passion, purpose, and path.

For now, we hope this chapter has been instrumental in assisting you in mapping out a career strategy to maximize the new world of work. Despite the constant media hype, there is an avalanche of work opportunities for professionals who are willing to think differently about their careers.

Never before have there been no boundaries and no limitations to career options. Using career personas, role-based hiring strategies, and Virtualpreneur training options, you can capitalize on the new world of work!

> *If you want something better, you have to be willing to do something different.*
>
> —Terri Maxwell

In the next chapter, we'll explore how new business models for the gig economy created a talent marketplace.

CHAPTER 8

New Business Models for the Gig Economy

In many ways, the basic business model in a market-driven economy has not changed much in the past two hundred years. However, as everyone now knows, the Internet changes everything; including the way we worked, and this occurred long before the pandemic reached our shores.

Business models that would be unsustainable without the Internet can become enormously successful when a service or product can be sold to millions of new customers with little overhead, almost no advertising expenses, and global distribution.

The gig economy is just that: a marketplace that is fueled by the fractionalized nature of work. The trends of the new world of work had already been responsible for replacing millions of worker incomes around the globe. The business models that supported and accelerated these trends, again *before* the pandemic, made it painfully obvious.

An Evolution

At the end of the 2000s, the move to Internet-enabled business/working models had begun, with industries like IT and graphic design taking the lead. As exponential technology growth dramatically increased capabilities, a growing list of industries relocated work to the virtual arena.

Even sectors like healthcare and education, which once seemed bounded by the walls of hospitals and classrooms, moved many functions to the cloud.

CROWDSOURCING WORK

The real distinction between traditional outsourcing and crowdsourcing is that the task or work is outsourced to the public at large rather than to paid employees or dedicated independent contractors.

In reference to the distributed work environment, the work can be fractionalized and assigned to a variety of workers for completion or problem solving.

Fractionalized work output can create a competitive advantage similar to having an all-star team of pro athletes, each with their own role to play.

The model to distribute work to various groups based on specialization or experience is not new, but the Internet-enabled crowdsourcing worked quickly, which sped up fractionalization. This opened the door to a global talent market, with its limitless boundaries. And this created what is now known as the gig economy. Today, someone can monetize his individual contribution based on work experience, passion, and education with just a mouse click, phone call, or text from a mobile device.

More importantly, when the contributions of others participating are bundled in a similar forum, fractionalized work output can create a competitive advantage similar to having an all-star team of pro athletes, each with their own role to play.

As the gig economy spread globally, based first on the fractionalization of work, and then on accessibility of work globally, new business models began to emerge to match gig workers with hiring companies.

When we wrote the first edition of *The New World of Work*, these platforms were relatively new. Today, they are readily available and driven by two factors:

- Skill and experience, from general to specialized

- Personalized selection/matching, from mass to curated

This grid represents a small fraction of the crowdsourced virtual work platforms matching both freelance and virtual talent in the gig economy.

VIRTUALPRENEUR™ PLATFORMS

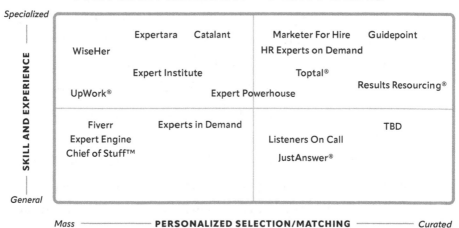

Source: Succeed On Purpose, 2021 study on Virtualpreneur platforms

COWORKING SPACES ACCELERATE THE GIG ECONOMY

> *As well as embracing the virtual work model, businesses must create physical spaces that can easily integrate to the virtual world to drive productivity and innovation.*
>
> —Dan Fallon, former vice president and
> chief technology officer, Navistar

When *The New World of Work* was published a decade ago, we understood that one of the barriers was where work would be performed. Would it be the home? Companies didn't seem ready to accept that. Would companies create micro-offices? Workers weren't open to that as a viable solution.

Enter WeWork. By 2014, WeWork was considered the fastest-growing coworking space, fueled in large part by its rapid, albeit unprofitable, growth. What WeWork understood was that workers wanted the community of coworking without the feeling of being trapped in a cube or office that required a thirty-minute commute.

As WeWork grew in popularity, many traditional companies embraced their model, leasing space in WeWork facilities to cater to a flexible work environment that a new generation of workers demanded.

Although WeWork almost imploded during its ill-fated 2019 IPO attempt, the company not only survived this tragic chapter of a unicorn-style company but repositioned itself to capitalize on the explosion of virtual work post-pandemic.

After the shockwaves of 2020 subsided, disrupting life and work globally, WeWork recognized that as companies came back online, many wanted to transition to a virtual or hybrid work model. WeWork created several flexible coworking offerings to make it easier for companies to support virtual staff.

Ironically, the companies that had leased space from WeWork and other coworking spaces were already well positioned to manage work globally and virtually. That meant that those companies were well prepared for virtual work, and they navigated the pandemic with less disruption.

What can we learn from this? Companies with the leadership and management team that can identify and recruit the workers, assemble fractional tasks to be completed, and deliver results *while* working virtually are significantly nimbler than those that are still struggling to make this shift.

One thing we know for sure is that the move toward virtual business models will continue, steadily building a global workforce and a talent marketplace.

Former British Prime Minister Winston Churchill famously said, "Those who fail to learn from history are doomed to repeat it." Using history as our guide, we should be able to predict what will happen in the future. By applying the rapid changes of technological advances, we can start to dream about what the future of the world will look like in ten, twenty, or thirty years.

One thing we know for sure is that the move toward virtual business models will continue, steadily building a global workforce and a talent marketplace.

The Home Agent Model

Working Solutions, Tim's first entrepreneurial venture, was one of the original pioneers of the home agent contact center model, leveraging a virtual workforce and technology to change the model. This model is now widely employed by businesses around the globe, providing businesses an ever-growing source of talent and giving talented workers the option of monetizing their skills without ever leaving their homes.

Leveraging the remote worker allowed Working Solutions to overcome the challenges presented from staffing limitations for dedicated, skilled workers. The model has exploded beyond the contact center and now includes all transactions and interactions that can be fractionalized in the cloud.

ARTIFICIAL INTELLIGENCE

In late 2015, with the gig economy changing yet again, Tim started Humach (Humans and Machines), combining a division from Working Solutions with agents that were full-time employees *with* the power of artificial intelligence. Tim's vision was that if you could combine virtual agents who were full-time gig workers with advancements in artificial intelligence, they could create significant value for customers via a more effective customer service solution.

The model precisely balances human talent and advanced technology to create tailor-fit customer service experiences for our clients' customers that are unparalleled. Today, Humach has served over two hundred successful clients and earned more than fifty awards for service and sales excellence.

Amazon Expands via the Talent Marketplace

Online retailer Amazon has one of those business models that would not be sustainable in the old economy. However, in the new world of work, it is effective because it creates a company with no boundaries. Amazon, in many ways, was the original pioneer of leveraging the dynamic in the retail space. Now it has divisions and initiatives dedicated to exploring the evolution of the model and the virtual platforms that have been built.

One such example was the Amazon Mechanical Turk (MTurk), a crowdsourcing Internet marketplace for work that enables computer programmers—known as "requesters"—to coordinate the use of human intelligence to perform tasks that computers are currently unable to do. The requesters were able to post *Human Intelligence Tasks* (HITs), such as choosing the best among several photographs of a storefront, writing product descriptions, or identifying performers on music CDs. Workers, who were called "providers," can then browse among existing tasks and complete them for a monetary payment set by the requester.

MTurk was the predecessor to many of the virtual work platforms that are commonplace today, and Amazon's creation of it signified a new business model, based on the fractionalization of work and globalization of talent.

This model led Amazon to rethink the concept of retail, and they soon offered "stores" that everyday people could open on the platform. Have a passion for gifts? Create your own Amazon gift store. Care about the environment? Not a problem, start a sustainable products shop. Want to resell books? Have your own virtual bookstore. The ways that Amazon has leveraged the new world of work are endless, primarily because they understand this new world and what fuels it.

For me, the real "wow factor" in the virtual model is the nimbleness/flexibility it offers. For example, we did a program for an 800 company and were able to staff (using an at-home model) for their peak time, minute-by-minute, because we had the staff ready and waiting! That kind of flexibility is a must in today's competitive global environment.

—Paulo Silva, vice president, Latin America, Xerox

Retooling Manufacturing

The near implosion of the automobile industry in the United States in 2010 hastened a trend that has been coming for many years: Old-style manufacturing is being retooled in a way that workers and their unions never thought possible. The basis for this reworking of the factory floor is the fractionalization of job tasks. The concept of "just-in-time inventory," which was a staple of planning in the automotive industry for decades, has been incorporated into the area of human resources.

The old way of staffing for manufacturing jobs has not been profitable for many years, but it took a near-collapse for the industry to realize that it must either change its way of doing business or it would be out of business. While it has been painful—change always is—the automotive industry is slowly moving into the new world of work.

In the old days, it was said that a service company's assets went up and down in the elevator each day. While today's talented workers may never set foot in a company elevator, skilled, motivated contributors are more important than ever before.

3D Printing: Now an Everyday Tool

At the time of the first edition, one of the biggest breakout technologies in *The New World of Work* was affordable, high-resolution 3D printers. Historically known as additive manufacturing, these three-dimensional printers mold objects out of wax or plastic working from digital configurations provided by software. They became a powerful tool for professional creators, hobbyists, and specialty manufacturers.

What was once a futuristic dream in science fiction is now an industrial-strength reality, and is now available in home offices. Virtualpreneurs can create almost any shape, geometric object, or feature by using a printer in your own office.

In 2012, our prediction for this disruptive technology was that it would drive an entirely new group of workers who could seize the means of design, rapid prototyping, fabrication, and production from large corporations.

And it did. Today, innovators are not only printing products, and Imagineering new product designs, they are printing everything from semiconductor chips to realistic artificial hands and human cells!

With *all* these new models, one constant is *change*. The companies that can equip their workforce to deal with an unending stream of change will succeed in the next decade. Specifically, a critical aspect of next-generation workforce is how they manage uncertainty and risk.

> *Executives who are exceptional at handling uncertainty and risk in the new world of work know their success is based on how they carry themselves as well as understand, process, and deftly perform in uncertain and risky situations. The litmus test*

is how they show up and respond in real time and points in the future.

—Dr. Ryan Lahti, strategic advisor to STEM organizations, contributor with Forbes Coaches Council, and founder of OrgLeader.com

The Trends Don't Lie

Prior to the pandemic, historians, futurists, political pundits, and many business leaders believed in the power of the gig economy. They agreed it could create an improved economic structure for both companies and workers, creating new business models in the process.

The pandemic just made this reality crystal clear to the rest of the world. What followed, the Great Resignation, was powered less by the pandemic, and more by the passion these new business models offered. Workers' demand for flexible and virtual roles became the last nail in the proverbial coffin for the old way of working.

Now, how can you, as a professional, benefit from the new world of work? First, fully commit to the model. Second, hire managers who understand how to compete for talent in a virtual environment. Third, build a technology infrastructure in the cloud capable of supporting your business.

History teaches us that the jobs created in the new world of work will demand different skills and an entrepreneurial spirit that will drive economic and job growth through innovation and an onslaught of new business models. Because work was fractionalized, it opened the door to a global talent *marketplace* readily available to anyone who wanted to rethink their career or adopt a new talent strategy for their organization.

Now that we've explored the global talent marketplace from the worker (supply side), let's turn our attention to the demand side of the equation—how companies can compete for virtual talent globally rather than from a fifty-mile radius of the corporate office.

So, where's Waldo (your next great hire) in this new marketplace? He could be anywhere in the world.

Talent Globalized

CHAPTER 9

Competing for Virtual Talent

Any HR executive or small business owner has experienced the sensation of being hit with a deluge of resumes after posting a position on a job board. In the good old days, companies took the time to review resumes, at which point the best of the applicants were invited to come in for more formal interviews.

This process took a lot of time and was ineffective the majority of the time. So, how difficult will it be when these applicants are virtual and global? Will it be more difficult to find the best person for the job?

In 2012, we believed it *would* be more difficult, and now ten years later, we're convinced of it. Jobs are left unfilled because companies with these roles can't find the workers who want them. This talent chasm is slowing economic recovery and limiting job recovery around the globe.

Most companies may not realize that there are now hundreds of virtual work platforms that exist for just about any job you can think of. Furthermore, many of the traditional employment recruiter forms are now offering recruiters to fill *both* full-time and freelance roles.

Imprimis Staffing, a well-known national recruiter, recognized before the pandemic that their customers wanted to hire both full-time workers and freelance talent to fill positions. They began to retool their firm to better serve customers and take advantage of this burgeoning global talent marketplace.

> *It makes sense for recruiting firms to offer a freelance option. Freelancers own their own businesses, pay their own expenses, file their own taxes, and generally act as a "consultant" to employers, therefore making it easy to use their skills and experience when you need it and not when you don't. Recruiting firms realize that, in addition to current and traditional services (temp, temp-to-perm, direct hire), a rapidly expanding freelance market that has grown exponentially during the pandemic cannot be ignored. Clients are desperately in need of talent, and the freelancer marketplace is one more way to secure that talent.*
>
> —Valerie Freeman, founder, Imprimis Staffing

Recruiting this new virtual talent will be the *currency* of the new world of work. What we can learn from the gig economy is to ask different questions. For example:

- How will you identify talent?

- How will you train and manage them?

- Should there be hard metrics for results and outcomes?

- What are the standards that we use to measure the new contingent workforce?

To help with these decisions, remember that there are three key characteristics that represent a successful virtual workforce, regardless of their employment classification (1099 or W-2). When contemplating hiring a virtual worker, these traits should be at the top of your list:

1. They should be skilled workers.

2. They must be flexible and adaptable.

3. They must be self-motivated.

Each of these traits is important on its own and they become critical when combined. Let's take a look at each characteristic and why they are important in the new global marketplace.

Skilled Workers

Qualifications are critical. Finding those who are most qualified will be the most effective strategy for fractionalized work. People with experience, education, training, and credentials will be able to compete in a virtual environment, marketing their specialization to the highest bidder. In many ways, this is a perfect market, and the world has become the marketplace.

> **In many ways, this is a perfect market, and the world has become the marketplace.**

The process of identifying qualified workers will require a new form or system of management. Managers must be able to identify the right skill set and design a results-based compensation structure to effectively leverage the virtual workforce. They must then direct specific work products to experienced workers with proven performance and reputation for results. Think of this as a social media approval rating for work performance. These will be objectives-based compensation structures with clearly defined measurement tools.

Flexibility

Flexibility is the key to talent acquisition in the new structure. If the key to motivating in the new world of work is flexibility, our organizations must learn to embrace the value of flexibility in order to retain top talent.

The value of the worker is to complete the task and fulfill a need. If you are working for a company and you fulfill their needs, you are a valuable employee, regardless of when or where the work is completed. The sooner you understand and embrace the new world of work, the sooner you will be at a competitive advantage.

Self-Motivation

What motivates the new workforce? Our research has now proven that the new model of a virtual contingent workforce suggests that there are both intrinsic (internal) and extrinsic (external) motivation factors that influence the contributions of the new contingent workforce.

- Intrinsic motivation comes from the enjoyment and feeling from the actual contribution and completion of the work itself. The secondary result is the sense of belonging to the social network, group, or community through individual participation and involvement.

- Extrinsic motivation includes the economic or monetary benefit of completing the work product or task. The form of currency will now take on a broader meaning, suggesting that there will be more than money motivating the new workforce. Social recognition is becoming a powerful extrinsic motivator, similar to social status of the past.

This new workforce places greater value on flexibility, individual contribution, work they are passionate about, and control of one's own destiny to succeed in the gig economy. Companies that capitalize on the new currency of these new workers will have a competitive advantage with a new labor-cost model.

CASE STUDY:

Elizabeth Eiss was consulting for businesses in 2011, and noticed her clients wanted to hire her freelance team. They would say, "How do I get a (insert freelancer name) for my business?"

At the time, she didn't realize that her superpower was finding great talent, so she initially offered to help them find freelancers off freelance job boards. However, she quickly realized that she had stumbled onto a major problem. Most businesses didn't have the time or compatibilities to assess freelancer profiles or interview to select the best talent. Boom, ResultsResourcing was born.

ResultsResourcing became *the* freelance platform that comes with your own recruiter. Their clients get the heart and hands of real human beings who find, interview and vet freelance talent, *plus* everything great about online job board platforms. Their mission is to be the trusted alternative to DIY job platforms for both employers and freelancers. For a small fee, ResultsResourcing matches client skill needs with Virtualpreneurs—and provides a choice of three vetted candidates in about three weeks.

Elizabeth noted: *"Platforms have transformed business opportunities for both sellers and buyers, creating a global market for virtual services. Platforms are a valuable source of market intelligence, provide models for new practitioners in areas of expertise, and help solve the access to market and marketing requirements to fuel a business.*

It can be hard to stand out on work platforms, and technology frameworks can limit the ability to zone in on the best job match. Said another way, it can be hard for a client to find the right freelancer and hard for the freelancer to find the right client. This results in wasted effort by employers with jobs and wasted time of freelancers who bid on work with limited likelihood of winning the job. That's why we created the ResultsResourcing Match Guarantee—to guarantee that we'll find that match for our clients."

As companies learn how to compete in the global talent marketplace, they need to better understand how to close the talent gap. Talent and workforce-development strategies should incorporate the gig economy preferences of the empowered worker in order to remain competitive.

The key to closing the talent gap is to think about talent and their *passion* for the work rather than location of the worker.

CHAPTER 10

Close the Talent Gap

Since the pandemic, companies have chosen to compete for talent by increasing compensation and making promises about flexibility and hybrid work models. Although this may be a good short-term fix, it's not sustainable, especially if there is a market correction.

What great companies understand is that the ultimate empowerment of tomorrow's workforce is *passion*, whether they are a freelancer, W-2 hourly staff, or salaried. Since the pandemic, workers are now demanding virtual work, as well as work they enjoy.

The fear most corporate executives have is that gig workers will do "side hustle gigs" while on the payroll. The truth is, they might. The solution isn't to legislate behavior, but rather to understand motivation. Why are they doing side hustles? Because of passion. They want to do things they are passionate about. The solution then is to match workers' passions to fractional roles—W-2 or 1099.

The ROI is enormous: an *agile workforce* that you can flex up or down as the needs of your business change; a *passionate workforce* that cares as much about your customers as you do; plus, one of the best secrets about this model is that it creates a *competent workforce* because they take care of their own training. The engaged, empowered worker is *so* passionate about his or her vocation and actively seeks training, knowledge, and skills to compete on their own terms.

The question is … how do you find them?

WHERE ARE THE WORKERS?

The biggest challenge for companies competing in the new world of work is finding talent that can move seamlessly across the gig economy. They are entrepreneurial by nature and demand flexibility and virtual work. If they think your full- or part-time role will require an office work or a commute, they won't even apply.

What does that mean to employers? When specific talent is a scarce resource and at a premium, we must expand our boundaries to include the global workforce who can work from anywhere, virtually.

The key to success in the new world is this: *flexibility!*

The most competitive companies are learning how to attract, hire, and retain the best talent; the most experienced and knowledgeable workers for the positions required. The key to success in the new world is this: *flexibility!*

New-world-of-work employees will work on their own terms, and they require a work/life balance as well as the ability to work remotely. A large part of their compensation is now based on flexibility, and the most competitive companies will master the art of creating a mobile workforce that can work from anywhere, *doing work they are passionate about.*

Offering remote work creates an opportunity to attract and retain the most qualified talent, allowing them to perform roles from anywhere in the world.

Identifying the right knowledge worker is the key to the future success of business, regardless of where the worker resides.

Creative CEOs can reduce overhead because you're only hiring for the skills you need at that time. Creating a variable cost model to support labor requirements will enable an on-demand labor force, improving margins for companies. Transferring fixed labor costs to variable costs will allow companies to reward skilled workers more for productivity, performance, and efficiency.

The best labor, full- or part-time, will ultimately demand more compensation in the marketplace because they deliver results and make an impact for the businesses they serve. It also means there is a need to organize work differently.

Organizing the Work

The virtualization of work requires technology that can support the skilled workforce. Companies must identify the people who possess the skills needed to support the work, as well as prepare management to support these workers.

The three key areas for organizing the work output are:

1. **Systems:** Back- and front-office technology infrastructures are required to capitalize on the virtual worker. Innovative and intuitive applications that facilitate effective and efficient work interactions and transactions will drive results in a virtual environment. Collaboration tools for individuals to share ideas will create innovation and efficiency. But more importantly, they will foster the psychological benefit of

being part of a team. Companies should never underestimate the purpose component of managing and measuring talent and ensuring their systems, processes, and organization are aligned to deliver on the promise.

2. **Talent:** We continue to reference "talent" in this book and do so very deliberately. The new world of work is all about access to talent. The ability to find the right individual with the right skill set for the right job is the reason the model will create market opportunities for the skilled worker who can compete in the virtual world. Embracing new cloud-based platforms, social media applications, and collaboration tools will allow individual workers to compete beyond the constraints of their previous four-walls employer. Convincing forward-thinking executives to focus on the output rather than the internal versus external resources will allow the educated, experienced, skilled worker to break down the barriers to attracting talent.

Workers now have to identify their own strengths, passions, and weaknesses, similarly to the way any business would, in order to compete. Statistically, individuals who are passionate about the work they do are not only open to learning new skills, but they also seek them out.

Beyond fractionalized work "units," the remaining full-time jobs are not the same jobs our parents once had. They require a different set of skills. Automation stripped off the routine, simple tasks, leaving a more complex interaction. Companies must recruit for a dynamic-thinking, skilled worker with the skills to deliver results.

The former General Manager of Major League Baseball's Oakland Athletics, Billy Beane, adopted a talent-evaluation program that is taken right out of *The New World of Work*'s playbook. In the book *Moneyball*, author Michael Lewis covers how the team, led by Beane, changed the way professional baseball players are chosen and compensated.

The book focuses on the team's analytical, evidence-based, saber metric (technical analysis of baseball) approach to assembling a competitive baseball team, despite Oakland's disadvantaged revenue situation. Using this new talent evaluation approach, the Athletics became a team that contended for the American League pennant while keeping its budget balanced.

Think of your talent strategy the way Billy Beane did. Create new metrics. Look for the right fit rather than the best people. Focus less on location and more on passion.

3. **Measurement:** New initiatives and measurement metrics are required to help design and build the organizational structures to support the virtual workforce. Empowering the new workforce actually *improves* results. When trust is incorporated into the employer/worker relationship, the emphasis becomes accomplishing the tasks and achieving results and outcomes. The focus will change, and results will follow.

In order for a virtual model to be successful, you have to trust employees out of the gate. It's like sending your children off to college; you have to trust that they'll make the right decisions and be successful.

—Jeanne Jones, global director job
seeker success, Indeed

Transform the Learning Experience

Training workers in this new environment requires a complete new set of tools. Most colleges are not yet (even today ten years later) well suited to train gig economy workers, which is why numerous training platforms have cropped up since we wrote the first edition of the book. These platforms, many of which both Succeed On Purpose and Humach partnered with, could erode the need for a traditional college education because the gig economy is powered by passion, and passion fuels the quest for a different type of knowledge.

There are three sets of tools we've found that are game changers to leaders managing next-generation talent in a world we can no longer predict. These platforms are built by thought leaders who transformed themselves and their own organizations, and they conducted extensive research studies to determine what created this transformation.

1. **The Leadership Scorecard from JumpCoach.com**

Scott Drake had been a technology executive for decades. Scott's journey into leadership was long, painful, and it took ten years to thrive as a leader and not feel like an imposter. When he became a leader of leaders, he saw next-generation leaders making the same mistakes and wrestling with the struggles. He began searching for a faster way to teach leadership. That search turned into a five-year research project and a mission to demystify leadership so it could be mapped, measured, and molded in such a way that leaders could advance their own skills, based on their unique perspectives.

In addition to building the Leadership Scorecard, Scott created a Leadership Accelerator platform and launched it through JumpCoach.com. It is truly one of the simplest, yet most powerful tool kits available to leaders who want to solidify leadership fundamentals to manage next-generation workers.

THREE-STEP PROCESS

There are three steps to becoming a complete leader

MINDSET

Great leaders think differently than great role players. They have detached their egos from being the expert and embraced being a leader.

SCORECARD

Complete leaders know what to observe and measure to know they're doing a great job. They know the game and the rules of the game.

WAYFINDING

There is no single right way to lead. Complete leaders are adaptable, lifelong learners who add needed skills in a just-in-time manner.

Source: JumpCoach.com

2. Positive Intelligence program from Shirzad Chamine

Shirzad Chamine is the author of the *New York Times* best-selling book *Positive Intelligence*. He has lectured on the Positive Intelligence program at Stanford University and trained faculty at Stanford and Yale business schools. In addition to his higher-ed achievements, Shirzad has been the CEO of the largest coach training organization in the world. A preeminent C-suite advisor, Shirzad has coached hundreds of CEOs and their executive teams. His background includes a BA in psychology, an MS in electrical engineering, and an MBA from Stanford.

Shirzad's Positive Intelligence program is based on research with more than five hundred thousand participants from fifty countries, including CEOs, students, elite athletes, and sales, operations, and technology teams.

Recent advances in functional MRI (fMRI), which measures how neural activity changes blood flow, have allowed scientists and psychologists to witness the real-time working of the brain for the very first time. That means scientists can now pinpoint the regions of the brain involved in producing different thoughts or feelings that either derail or create success. The breakthrough contribution of *Positive Intelligence* research uncovered the core factors that impact both performance and well-being.

3. The StillPoint Experience from Vista Caballo

Fast Company named Lisa Arie "the CEO whisperer." She works with mission-driven, people-centric CEOs and top performers to transform the people who are transforming the planet.

Lisa's research found that most people rely on only one of three different human intelligence systems, which significantly reduces their ability to solve problems. She created a science-based methodology so leaders can discover how to access, and rely on, all their intelligence systems as they solve challenges in real time. The results are as dramatic and immediate as the ROI.

As a Certified B Corporation Vista Caballo has been recognized as Best for the World by B Lab since 2015.

The StillPoint Experience is a scientifically validated, highly customized, blended learning and development system that harnesses the power of the group to solve real business problems in real time and develops your team in the process.

Passion Rules

When an engaged workforce specifically targeted for the job with the tools to be successful is unleashed, you have a recipe for success. By bringing in highly skilled workers for flex capacity or short-term assignments, you will be able to use variable-cost labor models to increase output and margins.

How do you position yourself or your firm to take advantage of the virtual workforce? Here are five steps:

1. Determine the skills required rather than the roles budgeted.

2. Evaluate if those skills should be contract/freelance or full time.

3. Define what Succeed On Purpose calls "fit attributes," which are the personality and character attributes that match your culture (regardless of whether the role is freelance or full time).

4. Define how to measure performance: from activity completion to work product delivered to results generated, the clearer the measurement, the more effective the result will be.

5. Ensure your recruiters have the connections to this new world and are hiring for skills and fit rather than experience and location.

Are location flexibility and passion/fit alignment crucial for successful companies to compete in the new world of work? We predicted they would be back in 2012, and today, it's becoming obvious to the rest of the world as well.

Regardless of your role, competing for talent in this new marketplace requires tapping into the motivation of Virtualpreneurs and gig workers around the globe. Although this can feel daunting, it's easier than you might think.

CHAPTER 11

Motivating Tomorrow's Workforce

The new world of work is a fundamental shift in the way people work, changing organizations and disrupting the manner in which businesses operate. It will continue to be a driving force in the global economy, enabling new forms of competition. Those who embrace it will thrive, while those who don't will become extinct.

As we learned about each of these trends—the fractionalization of work, the globalization of talent, and the virtualization of technology—we began to understand that although they are powerful trends unto themselves, they actually work together, like parts of a well-oiled machine.

Technology certainly blew up the barriers to work, but in many cases, it was the professionals who charted their own Virtualpreneur careers that ultimately *moved* work from the cube to the cloud.

Fractionalization is now possible because of the virtualization of technology and the globalization of talent. The virtualization of technology was driven, in large part, by the globalization of talent, made possible by the fractionalization of work.

Technology simultaneously enabled both the fractionalization of work and the globalization of talent, but it was the workers making a purposeful shift toward the benefits of a virtual career that *created* the talent marketplace.

Technology equipped the customer to be more demanding, which caused companies to think differently about keeping the best people to take care of this empowered customer. As new gig workers demanded to work on their own terms, we can now see that all of these factors—virtual technology, the empowered customer, and the Virtualpreneur—were already changing the way business was done by the time we wrote the first edition. Ten years later, the pandemic just made it crystal clear to the world.

To comprehend how to motivate tomorrow's workforce, where talent has been globalized, we must understand the willingness of the workforce to adopt this new model, as well as the marketplace that enabled it to occur before the pandemic.

There are three societal drivers that create the connection between the fractionalization of work and the gig economy:

1. **Motivation:** In 2012, there was already a burgeoning global talent pool driven more by quality of life than traditional compensation structures. The pandemic just caused the vast majority of workers to jump into this new marketplace. A worker's motivation has expanded to include not just flexible work from wherever they want, but fractionalized work they enjoy.

2. **Productivity:** This same global talent pool that demands high-quality work at decent wages had been equipped to work virtually, whether at home or in a coworking space, regardless of the origin of work. Not only are these workers more capable, but in many cases, they are more productive. A randomized study by researchers at Stanford University compared productivity rates of a company's on-site workers with remote workers. During the nine-month study, the researchers found a 12 percent increase in productivity for the at-home workers. Of that increase, 8.5 percent came from working more hours (due to shorter breaks and fewer sick days) and 3.5 percent came from more performance per minute. The researchers speculate this was due to quieter working conditions. Moreover, since the pandemic, numerous studies have shown that virtual workers are happier, more productive, and enjoy their work more.

3. **Market demand:** All markets move toward optimum efficiency. In 2012, we said that in the case of work, the new talent marketplace could enable companies to compete more efficiently. Today, it's less about competing in the global marketplace and more that your survival depends on it.

> *It's clear that—given the right qualifications and support—workers are more productive in home offices, often by several percentage points.*
>
> —Dan Bell, chairman and chief executive officer, Hampton Roads Innovation Collaborative

The combination of these drivers has powered the gig economy to be just that—its own talent marketplace.

To comprehend the nature of this passionate global workforce, let's explore the origins of productive work: the process of creating or producing value, also known as a *job*.

Just as the work performed satisfies a need for a business, the activity of *creating value* satisfies a need for the individual who performs the work. Work production also creates value for the individual completing the work: a *reward*. In the study of sociology, rewards are considered economic preference functions, because the preference for rewards is different for various population segments and these preferences change over time.

Flexibility and empowerment for workers now rank higher than monetary compensation in overall job satisfaction.

For gig economy workers, there is a different set of economic preferences than their predecessors who moved from the factory to the corporation and ultimately into the cube.

What does all that mean to you?

Since the beginning of history, free enterprise has traditionally dictated how societies would compete for jobs, but now there is another dimension.

Rather than COVID-19, it is this *empowered* workforce that is, in part, fueling the gig economy and this global talent marketplace. From this perspective, value is not only derived from completing the work, but also from the benefits the workers receive. Flexibility and empowerment for workers now rank higher than monetary compensation in overall job satisfaction, and smart employers are learning how to make that empowerment part of their corporate DNA.

Virtualpreneurs are willing to modify their compensation structures to match overall drivers of satisfaction. Now, the compensation construct has changed from wages and benefits to a total compensation snapshot that includes quality of life, flexible work (and location) roles, and advancement based on one's passions versus an imaginary management hierarchy.

Next-generation compensation structures now create a new way of thinking about work based on a free market system. This lends itself well to the trend toward fractionalization.

The Next-Generation Motivation Models

Typically, people work most of their adult years. This is what we are taught at a young age and what we generally plan to do until retirement. Today, most professionals know that—for better or worse—permanent job security is a thing of the past. It is, in part, the absence of security that has shifted workers' mindsets over the last decade. This has resulted in our economic preferences changing from working for the security a corporation could provide to working on our own terms. This freedom is now what drives and motivates the new, global workforce with no boundaries.

According to the crowdsourced reference tool Wikipedia, employment is the contract between two parties where, in return for compensation, the employee contributes labor and expertise to an endeavor of an employer and is usually hired to perform specific duties, which in turn are packaged into a job. While this definition of employment is still accurate, the concept of an "employee" has changed to that of a trusted "team member." These are not false platitudes to make workers feel better. Successful, best-in-class companies integrate gig economy talent with their full-time management staff.

The dot-com bust, the terrorist attacks on September 11, 2001, the Great Recession of 2009, and the COVID-19 pandemic forced many workers to question their priorities.

Many professionals realized they were working for people who didn't care for them and were performing jobs they didn't enjoy in order to chase an elusive sense of security that was already an illusion. Today, most of these professionals decided they want more control of their future. As a result, their economic preference changed from *security* to *freedom*.

> **Today's workers are now loyal to the skills they can monetize, not the companies they work for.**

When this happened, the seeds that form the new world of work were planted. Today's workers are now loyal to the skills they can monetize, not the companies they work for.

Since we wrote the first edition over a decade ago, this shift toward freedom and passion created a workforce that dictates how their knowledge and skills will be packaged and sold in the gig economy that they are learning how to leverage.

As technology further enabled their freedom (more on that in the next section), they've been able to move from the cube to the cloud and leverage virtual employment opportunities, from anywhere in the globe. Again, this was occurring before the pandemic. In the process, gig talent learned to market themselves to the highest bidder and work at the time of their choosing.

So, it's not just the unavailability of positions that is fueling the gig economy. Worker motivation has changed, and more professionals are choosing to take control of their destinies. Freedom is the new currency for this workforce, while many corporations cling to a deceptive portrayal of "secure" wages and benefits.

> *Younger people especially are demanding more freedom in the workplace; there is no place for a nine-to-five schedule in their lives. Smart employers will give them the tools and flexibility they need to succeed personally and professionally, knowing team members will reward them with their best work.*
>
> —Jeff Puritt, president and chief executive officer, TELUS International

To understand the new universe, one must grasp that virtual workers' *motivation* changed. The originators of virtual work platforms like ResultsResourcing and Upwork understood from the beginning that the old corporate carrot-and-stick motivation models would not be effective with the new, empowered workforce.

In fact, some would contend that the carrot-and-stick model of motivation—where there is a promise of reward and a threat of punishment—never really worked because employees just found more effective ways to avoid responsibility. Regardless, the old-school tactic is completely ineffective with the current workforce.

Unlike previous generations, who dreamed of joining a company directly out of school or college and staying until retirement, today's workers are absolutely certain that their current employer will not be their last. In fact, job search site JobList found that 73 percent of all workers were considering quitting their job in 2021 and 2022. In addition, according to Gallup's 2021 State of the Global Workplace, only 15 percent of employees are engaged in the workplace.[17]

But worker motivation is only one part of the machine. As mentioned, there are three drivers that create a 360-degree connection between the fractionalization of work and virtualization of careers. They are:

1. A global talent pool motivated by quality of life and passion

2. A global talent pool that leverages virtual technology to attract high-quality work at decent wages

3. A new work marketplace that creates value by breaking work into smaller units (fractionalization) and leverages supply and demand

All these factors collided at once, which in turn meant that our world could experience a global pandemic and recover relatively quickly by historical standards.

This suggests that whatever reward is promised must be tied to short-term objectives. As for the stick, threats of punishment are not as effective if an employee is in the mindset of moving on. This situation results in a workforce with little or no loyalty, as well as no sense of commitment to building the enterprise. Remember what we mentioned earlier, today's worker is loyal to the skills he can monetize, not the employer.

---

17   "State of the Global Workplace," Gallup, 2017, https://www.fundacionprolongar.org/
       wp-content/uploads/2019/07/State-of-the-Global-Workplace_Gallup-Report.pdf.

What Happened to the Clock?

Adapting to an empowered workforce will be a critical requirement for businesses to be competitive. If a company's leaders fail to recognize, embrace, and prepare their managers for it, they will be left behind.

Gone are the days of militaristic management styles dictated by control and intimidation. How do executives manage motivation in a virtual environment? Simply put, tie rewards directly to employees' intrinsic motivations—their sense of empowerment and enjoyment.

> *The next generation of professionals is wired differently and has different priorities. Young people have no use for the inefficiency of a commute or the limitations of the cube. Culturally, they were born into a virtual world and instinctively know how to maximize virtual collaboration tools to be effective virtually. If companies want to remain relevant to this next generation of talent, they will have to build a strategy that includes virtual work.*
>
> —Tammy Valdez, former senior
> vice president, LifeLock

As an employer, prepare your management team to embrace the empowered workforce by focusing more on the passions of the worker rather than the management of work.

Here are some tips for focusing more on the passions of the new worker:

- Ask yourself what the traits are for identifying management talent in your business. Virtual managers need to possess the ability to identify and interact with individual mentors for leadership, management, and knowledge guidance.

- Identify the right individual with the right skill set, experience, and knowledge, and then establish clear objectives to be met.

- Manage and reward the results, production, and outcomes, not the time put into the work. Self-motivated success of the freelance workforce is the new reward for efficiency, productivity, and quality.

- Consider what management should look for in the empowered worker.

The key to managing this new workforce is to focus on their motivations and their passion for their work rather than the time spent doing the work.

How to Recognize an Empowered Worker

Empowered workers universally share several attributes, which enable the fractionalized, virtual quality of the new world of work. They are:

1. **self-starting**—they have the ability to self-motivate and accomplish the task or achieve the objective;

2. **educated**—they've gained critical knowledge in school, trade, or by developing street smarts;

3. **technologically savvy**—they have the ability to navigate through today's connected world;

4. **committed**—they are survivors who will not stop until they achieve success; and

5. **connected**—they are part of a team or network or willing to join one.

In the new world of work, the bar has been raised. Skilled workers no longer need to live within a fifty-mile radius of your company, which means companies have the nation or the world as their recruiting pool.

To the smart corporation, that translates into an ability to attract and retain the best talent from *around the globe.*

But even with no boundaries, there will be a shortage of skilled, knowledgeable workers, and the best talent will go not only to the highest bidder, but to the best platforms for empowered work. These will be organizations that truly understand this new frac-

> **The number of skilled, performance-based workers will grow at an unprecedented rate because of the globalization and fractionalization of work.**

tionalized, virtualized workforce and focus on inspiring and motivating rather than managing and legislating.

The number of skilled, performance-based workers will grow at an unprecedented rate because of the globalization and fractionalization of work.

Remember, it is not only about compensation; other intangible benefits are at play. More importantly, educating managers to identify talent and embrace the virtual workforce is a requirement for managing the new talent pool of empowered workers.

Equipping Businesses to Compete for Talent

If you own a small or medium business, the new work environment is very good news for you. While it's true that the fundamental strength of our economic future rests in the hands of entrepreneurs and small businesses across the nation, it is imperative that business leaders learn how to design a virtual talent strategy to maximize the fractionalization of work. This will ensure business productivity and efficiency as costs are managed variably during growth spurts.

Frequently, businesses are hampered by the absence of a scalable talent strategy. They ask themselves questions like, Where will we find talent? Who will be qualified? How can I afford the talent I need? These are the questions that keep most small business leaders awake at night. On one hand, they know they need talent to compete. But on the other hand, they are afraid to make mistakes or incur the expense of securing the best talent.

That is precisely why gig economy work platforms that also include a recruiter, and recruitment firms that recruit both full-time and contract roles, are key to your small business arsenal.

A virtual workforce is a great benefit to a small-to-medium-sized business like ours. About 70 percent of our workforce is virtual, which means we can recruit from a much larger talent pool. While we're based in Chicago, our people live in lots of different communities. So, we get the best talent, and they get to work from wherever they call home.

—Jeff Furst, president and chief
executive officer, FurstPerson

What's the next frontier for employee benefits? Earned wage access (EWA). All businesses now can increase employee recruitment and retention with innovative technology. The need for financial wellness benefits has never been greater. With employees being pulled in all different directions by economic uncertainty, it's up to employers to provide them with the tools they need in order to stay focused and productive at work. In turn, a more engaged workforce results in happier customers, broader efficiencies, and, ultimately, a healthier bottom line.

Immediate, one of the largest earned-wage instant-pay-access providers in the country, partners with employers to provide their employees with wages that have been earned but not paid whenever they are needed. With innovative financial wellness technology like Immediate, offering earned wage access is helping reduce stress by providing a financial safety net for the workforce. Many employees find themselves turning to high-interest predatory loans or credit cards when unexpected expenses arise in between paydays. Payday lenders charge usurious rates (upward of 600 percent APR in some states) that create cycles of debt that are nearly impossible to escape. Compounding the problem is inflation and the rapidly increasing cost of living, which is placing an even heavier financial burden on our workforce, regardless of income level and socioeconomic status.

> *By providing employers with no-cost benefits like Immediate, managers can spend less time worrying about financial stress impacting their team's job performance and more time focusing on improving output. As distractions climb to an all-time high, it is important for businesses to be mindful of how they can help create a more productive environment so their employees can thrive both professionally*

> *as well as personally, whether working remote or in-office.*
>
> —Matt Pierce, founder and chief
> executive officer, Immediate

Based on a recent Immediate survey, 75 percent of employees believe that access to earned wages will alleviate their financial stress, and 82 percent of employees say they are more engaged at work since their company began offering Immediate. Arming your team with access to earned wages builds loyalty while simultaneously improving productivity … a win-win benefit for employers and employees alike.

Stimulating the businesses that make up a substantial part of our economy means it will be even more important to fuel the new contingent workforce by encouraging a system of risks and rewards. By nurturing the innovation of this workforce and treating them as entrepreneurs, we thus can share the notion of risk and reward, which is the basis of entrepreneurship. If this is accomplished, we will accelerate the adoption of *The New World of Work*'s model.

The Five Ms for Managing a Virtual Team

There are as many ways to motivate a virtual team as there are teams. However, we have identified five important strategies for managing a virtual team. These are:

1. **model**—set and communicate the objectives so everyone understands the objectives;

2. **methods**—obtain the right technologies and define the processes and methodologies for success;

3. **metrics**—develop the right objectives for task-related processes and functions that can be completed on time;

4. **measure**—monitor the performance to ensure quality work; and

5. **motivate**—finding the passion for the individual and teamwork is key. Look for opportunities to socialize, interact, and set the culture.

So, what do you want to do today? Where will you work from today? Whether you work at the office, car, home, hotel, pool, beach, relative's house, airport, or restaurant, the new world of work is the most efficient, flexible, and productive environment in the history and evolution of work.

The new world of work is the most efficient, flexible, and productive environment in the history and evolution of work.

Regardless of your strategy for finding global talent, the gig economy provides unlimited options for rethinking your talent strategy, all because the fractionalization of work and the power of a global talent marketplace, which removed the boundaries of work.

Without boundaries, new competitive models are free to evolve. To evolve, technology must continue to enable the workforce, increasing its productivity and access to knowledge and information.

To grasp the productive power of virtualized technology, it's important to explore how many companies tapped into the gig economy to survive and *thrive* in a post-pandemic world, especially as companies face inflation, a global recession, and a workforce that beats to a different drum. Ironically, the key to winning in this brave new world is to go back to the basics—superior customer service.

SECTION 4

Technology Virtualized

CHAPTER 12

The Customer Service Revolution

To truly understand the origins of virtual work, customer service must be explored. Customers are constantly evolving and are increasingly more demanding. It was, in part, because of their demands that virtual, remote-agent customer service was born.

Fractionalized Work Serves the Customer

The best part of the fractionalization of work is that it aligns a business's motivation, enhanced customer service, with the empowered workforce's ability to *compete for work* based on its ability to provide exemplary customer experience. Think about that for a second: as a business executive, you can combine fractionalized work with a virtual workforce that can compete and work toward the same objectives that make companies more competitive. Fractionalized work in this new world is the ultimate way to build a service legacy that a business can leverage.

Presently, technology is enabling new service models. Understanding the new customer in a multichannel world requires all companies to rethink customer experience. Purchase decisions are now made with an abundance of information available on the product or service, as well as the reputation of the company, its brand, and its approach on how it treats the customer.

In early commerce, purchase decisions were made on the convincing presentations of the salesmen. Later, radio and television permitted companies to build brand equity through media outlets with advertising campaigns so powerful they could overcome product flaws or shortcomings. Do you remember the early television shows and commercials in the 1950s and 1960s, when customers were comfortable with their purchase decisions simply because everything was brought to them by some large company? Next came product placements in movies and sitcoms.

Today, social media and the exchange of information are so instantaneous, consumers have an overabundance of real-time, detailed opinions and customer feedback on any product or service. If the product or service does not live up to the claims or expectations, the entire world knows—in real time!

A competitive focus on the customer is now required to secure, retain, and build customer profiles and preferences. Personalization is now key, and today's customer has high expectations and demands skilled, experienced, knowledgeable support through any channel they decide to use to reach your company. This means that your customer service must be available 24/7, 365 days, through any channel (voice, email, chat, text, or social media) that your customer chooses to use.

In order to provide that, businesses need to tap into workers who are *motivated* by their passion for service and their willingness to be the best servants. That's part of the new world of work!

Embracing the Multichannel, Connected World

Many companies are inundated with technological enhancements to ensure they are competitive in the new multichannel, customer-centric world. Some simply stick their heads in the sand, while others are leapfrogging ahead. Instead of worrying about the effects of a multichannel, connected world, why not embrace it? Companies that embrace the change will become the leaders and own the market share.

What does that mean to you as a businessperson?

Forward-thinking executives understand that the newly empowered customer will decide what companies control the market share over the next decade. Customer experience has become the central nervous system of the new wave of e-commerce companies. What is the ultimate expression of complete customer satisfaction?

Customer experience has become the central nervous system of the new wave of e-commerce companies.

First-contact resolution and knowledgeable representatives who are empowered to make decisions. Together they define the ultimate expression of customer service.

Companies today need to provide employees with whatever they need to succeed. That means they'll always have the right tools, including the most up-to-date technology in the industry, along with consistent management support, and be empowered to use their skill and know-how to make immediate decisions.

What defines the culture of tomorrow's corporate leaders? Customer centricity, entrepreneurial spirit, innovation, and tapping into the new empowered workforce. There are several very successful early adapters to this customer model. No doubt, you likely use some or all of them every week. These innovative companies have cracked the code of customer experience in the NWoW.

Pay attention to this word of warning: there have been hundreds of studies over the years that found interactions from customers with negative or uninformed employees would drive customers to your competitors, so the reverse will work to your advantage. If you embrace the requirement and demand for better customer experiences in today's multichannel, connected, seamless world, you can grow market share and retain customers for life.

How do you deliver on customer expectations? By tapping into the passion, skills, and knowledge of the workforce and creating engaged workers. Secure and train engaged workers and empower them to make decisions, and you will build market share and keep customers.

The most interesting research on e-commerce was a study conducted by several Fortune 200 companies that once thought self-service was the path to save expenses and increase profits. The conclusion is that having customers serve themselves resulted in a reduced average order value of 5–15 percent. Why? Because an engaged, trained, dynamically thinking agent representing your product or service will ask the right questions, educate, inform, and ultimately sell more product. Now product or service knowledge workers can represent your brand and improve your conversion rate, top-line revenue. and bottom-line profit. By the way, they can work anywhere in the world as long as they are educated, experienced, and trained.

David Litman, cofounder of Hotels.com and Getaroom.com, has proven that he understands the customer better than most executives, and as such is a great role model for our examination of the NWoW. Litman is a pioneer in the online travel industry, having cofounded Hotel Reservations Network, which later became Hotels.com. As CEO of Hotels.com, he was responsible for building the world's largest hotel e-commerce website from start-up to the final sale to Expedia.

Prior to cofounding Hotels.com in 1991 with friend Robert Diener, Litman was an attorney who decided that he would rather be an entrepreneur. Changing occupations and professions is also part and parcel of the new world of work. Wanting to cater to his entrepreneurial spirit, he started a discount airline business in 1984 that became a multimillion-dollar wholesale airfare consolidation operation. In 1991, Diener and Litman saw the untapped potential in the hotel industry, and with an investment of only $1,200, the two founded what became Hotels.com. They sold their interest and left the company in 2004. Then, in 2008, they started Getaroom, a new hotel-booking website focusing on handpicked hotel deals in major cities. True to their form, it has become extremely successful too. Getaroom sold to Booking Holdings (Nasdaq:BKNG) on December 30, 2021, for $1.2 billion.

Driving the Customer Conversation

Talkdesk, one of the world's leading providers of customer service and cloud contact center software, is on a mission to intelligently unlock the promise and potential of great customer experiences. Tiago Paiva, the company's founder and chief executive officer, emphasizes that customer experience is key to the success of any business and one of the strongest competitive differentiators. In fact, he says, many consumers consider a company's customer experience just as important as the quality of its products and services.

Technology innovations like self-service, automation, AI, and omni-channel capabilities have given consumers a taste of the possibilities and raised the bar for customer service even higher. Some of the necessities of operating during the pandemic also resulted in advances with more touch-free, convenient services. Prevailing expectations now require fast, frictionless service from any device, anytime, and through any channel. According to Paiva, these increased expectations are prompting companies to focus more on transforming their contact centers and empowering contact center agents.

It's no secret, however, that call center agent attrition rate has long been a thorn in the side of many businesses. The effects of the Great Resignation are compounding the problem. Additionally, while organizations have realized benefits from equipping their contact center teams to work remotely, including access to a wider talent pool and boost in agent morale, obstacles remain.

According to recent Talkdesk research, 61 percent of organizations plan to adopt a hybrid work model permanently, but cite performance management, training, and onboarding as among the top challenges of a hybrid approach. To address these, 78 percent of customer experience professionals say they will prioritize investment in workforce engagement management tools.[18] Paiva sees this as a clear signal that employee demand for flexibility and work-life balance is being taken seriously by business leaders. Moreover, with growth projections for the cloud contact center market expected to reach as high as $50 billion in five years, the emphasis on workforce recruitment and engagement should be a welcome sign for agents and an arrow in the quiver of companies aiming to deliver superior customer experiences.

It all starts with having the right contact center technology and tools to engage agents, help them derive greater satisfaction from their work, and become more effective in serving customers. Providing stellar customer service is next to impossible if the agent is limited by antiquated, on-premises contact center technology and has to juggle between applications, work with disjointed apps, or search for information. By automating routine, mechanical tasks, agents can focus instead on solving complex customer problems or adding greater value through personalization and upselling.

"Sales, marketing, customer success, and customer service are converging to deliver more value and increase revenue," explains Paiva. "Well-trained agents with the right tools have the power to transform the contact center into a profit center, leveraging interactions to drive sales. This elevates the role of agents and positions them as drivers of bottom-line results for the organization."

Smart companies will seize the opportunity to leverage these emerging strategic assets. Happy agents make happy customers, and happy agents slow turnover. With AI-infused, easy-to-use tools, improved training, gamification, recognition, and incentives, agents will be well armed to create meaningful and memorable customer interactions.

---

18   "The Future of Workforce Engagement: The Rise of the Hybrid Contact Center," Talkdesk, September 2021, https://www.talkdesk.com/resources/infographics/the-future-of-workforce-engagement-the-rise-of-the-hybrid-contact-center/.

The Secret to the Service Revolution

The late founder of Walmart, Sam Walton, was ahead of his time in many ways, especially in his commitment to customer service. He was fond of saying, "The goal of the company is to have customer service that is not just the best but legendary." In the new marketplace, this type of attention to customer service details isn't just important, it's a matter of life or death for companies competing for the customer's share-of-wallet.

Today, customers enact commerce without driving to big brick-and-mortar facilities such as Walmart. Instead, they can shop while sitting at home or having a cup of coffee at Starbucks. The "always-on-and-always-open" commerce world has arrived and become the foundation for the next generation. In fact, it is all young people have ever known. The Internet has created the multichannel, digital world where everything from goods to services is a mouse click or mobile device tap away.

What does this mean to you and to the companies that want to compete in the new world of work? For one thing, you *must* adapt to the new demands of the next-generation, empowered customer. To do that, you must adapt the way you think about the next-generation worker.

> *At Office Depot / OfficeMax, we think about our business from an omni-channel perspective, and this approach has caused us to increase our focus on customer service relative to our e-commerce strategy. We asked ourselves, "How would our store personnel respond if a customer was searching for a product and couldn't find it?" From that point of view, we engineered both reactive and proactive customer service responses for our web-based customers. This is critical because no matter how*

good your web experience is, some customers will always require human intervention to best serve their needs.

Strategically, we found that as more customers moved their purchases to the web, it created the need for a different type of human service experience. It's clear that transactions can best be served by the web, but smart brands know that human interaction is an important way to differentiate themselves while providing a satisfying and memorable customer service experience.

—Tim McGrath, former senior vice president, customer service, Office Depot

This entire chapter was designed to make one critical point: empowered customers will respond best to empowered workers. Tap into the motivations of virtual workers who want to compete for *your* business, and you will tap into the nirvana once imagined in business fairy tales: laborers, who compete for the work you offer, will ensure that they take care of your crown jewels. They will, in turn, equip you to compete for your customer. This is the best part of the new world of work. The brightest, most talented virtual workers will compete for work they enjoy. So, you need to make the work something they enjoy and pay them for performance, which taps into their motivation. Then they will want to compete for your business by ensuring that your customers are loyal to your business. That's the promise of the future.

And this competition for talented workers will open new worlds of opportunity for skilled professionals.

CHAPTER 13

Creating a Productive, Tech-Enabled Workforce

A simple glance around the subway station, coffee shop, or restaurant illustrates the societal influence technology has had on our world. In locations around the globe, people sit gazing at their smartphone, iPad, or laptop. They check emails, text friends, use social networks, or watch YouTube videos and consume goods/services from web-enabled devices. For better or worse, we are all connected wirelessly.

> *There is a cultural shift underpinning this new workforce. The next generation of workers is naturally mobile, and technology enabled. They are more comfortable online than they are in cubes and are well suited for virtual work.*
>
> —Jim Milton, chief executive officer, Anthology, Inc.

These technological advances have certainly propelled the transformation and evolution of the workforce and workplace. The members of Generation Y have grown up in a digital world, immersed in technology in every aspect of their lives. Work, play, and all time in-between have equally converged, as our days are increasingly filled with multichannel, digital or virtual worlds that have become the real world.

In 2012, International Data Corporation estimated that there would be hundreds of millions of smartphones sold worldwide and more than two billion users connected via networks of high-speed access. Since life has dramatically changed with the digital revolution, it is a natural progression that the way the world works will also change with a completely wired, digital workforce. In 2022, only ten years later, the number of people that own a smart and feature phone is 7.26 billion, making up 91.54 percent of the world's population.

Digitally Wired Recruits That Produce

Several factors enabled the virtual workforce and radically improved productivity in the process. According to Forrester research company, "The growth of consumer broadband Internet (56 percent of US households have broadband in 2012, up from 10 percent in 2002) has enabled more employees to work from home."[19] As of April 2022, there were five billion internet users worldwide, which is 63 percent of the global population. Of this total, 4.65 billion are social media users.

In fact, according to an Upwork study, one in four Americans, which is over 26 percent of the American workforce, will be working

---

19   Sally Cohen, "Top Consumer Broadband Trends for 2008," Forrester, January 28, 2008, https://www.forrester.com/report/top-consumer-broadband-trends-for-2008/RES43885.

remotely through 2022.[20] They also estimate that 22 percent of the workforce (36.2 million Americans) will work remotely by 2025. As companies streamline virtual workforces to focus on what differentiates them, they must form deep partnerships with suppliers, partners, and customers while conducting work in distributed, virtual teams.

On many levels, the virtual call center was the first influential factor that led the work movement back toward distributed teams. It was followed by software development, then project management, then administrative work, and soon even knowledge-based work moved into the cloud, which positioned work to be accessed remotely.

Again, this movement was driven by both workers' demands for freedom and customers' demands for better service experiences from corporations. Customer service truly drove the enablement of cloud-based work because customers can demand a premium service experience at

Most companies understand that in today's customer-centric, social-media enabled world, they must compete by delivering a higher-quality customer experience from their happy and productive staff rather than focusing solely on the cost of their service enterprise.

a fraction of the cost. As companies like Amazon and Zappos.com began to chart a new course in the definition of a superior customer service experience, other companies followed suit once they figured out how to get their workers productive and engaged.

---

20 Adam Ozimek, "Economist Report: Future Workforce," Upwork, accessed November 22, 2022, https://www.upwork.com/press/releases/economist-report-future-workforce.

Today, most companies understand that in today's customer-centric, social-media enabled world, they must compete by delivering a higher-quality customer experience from their happy and productive staff rather than focusing solely on the cost of their service enterprise. In our business, we see firsthand how forward-thinking executives that understand engaged, empowered workers actually improve customer experiences. The residual effect is also obvious: companies that deliver the best branded customer experience will also control the market share in their industry.

Times Have Changed—for the Better

In the late 1980s, IBM built a 500,000-plus square-foot office park in Westchester, NY, to house thousands of employees. It was a place where the workers would commute to work, park their cars in massive parking lots, and assume their eight-to-five jobs in their cubes, thousands and thousands of cubes.

Then, in 2009, IBM started to shift meetings to a new, virtual meeting place, Second Life. Second Life users can work, socialize, and participate individually or together in groups in literally all aspects of the real world. These capabilities gave IBM the power to shift meetings and work to a virtual office complex.

Today, the IBM Westchester office complex is a ghost town. It's an empty shell reminding us of the old Industrial-Age organizations of days gone by and the old office park. Since the pandemic started in mid-March 2020, IBM has had 95 percent of their global workforce working remotely across 175 countries. Organizations around the world have experienced the pandemic and its employment impacts differently, but all have embraced working virtually in order to continue operations.

Now digital office complexes allow organizations to work anywhere and still be connected to the team rather than being isolated at home and away from peers and colleagues. Today's workforce can work anywhere at any time, while maintaining productivity from homes, cars, hotels, and anywhere they have connected access, but now in the *real* world.

IBM chairman and CEO Arvind Krishna commented on a post-pandemic prediction that said, "80 percent of the company's employees may stay in hybrid roles indefinitely, spending at least three days a week, maybe not all eight to ten hours, but at least some fraction of those three days, in the office."

Krishna said "10 to 20 percent of employees could potentially stay fully remote," but that he worried "about what their career trajectory was going to be."

New social networks are not only for personal use. In an effort to keep employees engaged and happy, businesses are embracing them at a faster rate than the adoption of any previous technology since the personal computer. In fact, a recent survey by Manta, an online small-business community, shows over 90 percent of small businesses now use some form of social media.

The evolution of technology and connected social networks has reversed the feeling of alienation or loneliness when working remotely, recalling John Donne's quote from 1624, "No man is an island." Virtual workers do not thrive when isolated from others; they want to be connected. Collaboration and engagement are now more important than ever.

What does all this mean in terms of the skills you, as a new professional, must now bring to the global talent table?

NEXT-GENERATION WORK PRODUCT

The number of skills required for specific work products has increased, and the digital revolution has created a connected network of knowledgeable employees capable of working wherever and whenever they want, as long as they complete tasks or achieve desired outcomes and results. And as expected, this flexibility leads to increased productivity. As noted, fractionalization results when routine work is broken down into smaller units or tasks. As this increasingly occurs among businesses around the globe, companies will hire fewer full-time workers and outsource routine jobs as contract projects.

INTELLIGENT WORKLOAD DISTRIBUTION

New software-routing engines now enable companies to take advantage of a skilled virtual workforce by optimizing the business work streams or transactions and route to the worker best suited to complete. Omni-channel contact center and CRM software providers have created Intelligent Workload Distribution (iWD), which takes customer service delivery beyond the contact center by tracking, prioritizing, and routing tasks to help companies meet customer demands and improve efficiency.

By prioritizing the work tasks and routing to the best people suited to handle the transaction and task, work products can be routed and distributed in a virtual environment to the most qualified, skilled individual.

Intelligent Workload Distribution enables enterprise-wide customer service delivery, provides greater business efficiencies, and improves customer service by enabling users to quickly define priorities and service levels in real time—based on the business value of each task.

By optimizing the business work streams and enabling service delivery outside the contact center, workload management software takes the effort out of the customer service experience by ensuring that the right person does the right work at the right time to meet customer expectations.

When you combine powerful software routing engines in the cloud that can fractionalize work products with a global workforce of specialized agents, you are maximizing the potential benefits and efficiency gains of the NWoW model.

> *Success in the new workplace is about making silos disappear. Companies need systems that push work to people with the right skill sets based on business priorities, regardless of where they sit in the organization. That means organizations need to understand skills, and how they overlap, for everyone—contact center, back office, branches, and the corporate headquarters staff. When this occurs, the efficiency gains are huge.*
>
> —Brad Baumunk, BPO expert and
> contact center consultant

Technology Is the Game Changer

As CEOs of companies and managers of workforces of talented professionals, we have witnessed up close and personal the changing face of the new world of work. We see this book as our chance to pass on what we've learned about navigating through this new territory—which we believe houses the most important economic transformation in our lifetime. This new paradigm is the most important economic change we've seen in our generation.

As you contemplate navigating the new world of work, there are four key things to consider:

1. How to grasp the ever-changing landscape of technology

2. How to close the talent gap in your business

3. How to rethink your own personal career strategy

4. And the power of the *why*

Technology has now enabled the worker in ways that revolutionize entire industries. Talent, skills, experience, and knowledge can now be monetized anywhere in the world. Virtualization has become a game changer in the world of IT for every business, and it is laying the groundwork for the new world of work evolution. Since IT has recognized the benefits of efficiencies and capabilities never possible in the brick-and-mortar facility, the marriage of virtualization and the contingent workforce is now complete.

> *The number-one benefit of information technology is that it empowers people to do what they want to do. It lets people be creative. It lets people be productive. It lets people learn things they didn't think they could learn before, and so in a sense, it is all about potential.*
>
> —Steve Ballmer, former chief executive officer, Microsoft Corporation

As technology continues to evolve, artificial intelligence will provide increasingly automated tasks, leaving the more complex, dynamic-thinking tasks to humans. This will require a more qualified and skilled knowledge workforce than ever before. Just as the Industrial Revolution automated the manufacturing industry, creating specialized machine operators, the Knowledge Revolution will require specialized skill sets to complete the tasks and run the *AI technology machines* of the future.

As an employer, in order to compete for talent, you must have the best technology and tools for your workforce. More importantly than ever before, your tools must be able to integrate with other tools with minimal effort. Gone are the days when everyone ran proprietary software; now all applications need the ability to integrate and work together based on standards: a communication and transaction network where everyone and everything is fully connected and working together, virtually.

What are the required technologies for the future of work?

1. High-speed access

2. Minimum computing requirements

3. Collaboration (communication tools)

4. Cloud-based applications (virtualization and grid networks)

5. Mobile (ties them all together)

HIGH-SPEED ACCESS

Broadband or high-speed Internet access is probably the single most important contributing factor to virtualization and the global workforce. It literally connects the world within milliseconds so people like you can collaborate and communicate in real time, regardless of where you are located.

Former AT&T chief executive officer Randall Stephenson once commented on the need for more connectivity, saying, "Fully one-third of all Americans don't subscribe to high-speed Internet access at all." AT&T is "trying to find a broadband solution that is economically viable to get out to rural America, and we're not finding one, to be quite candid."

How will America and the world be able to compete for global talent if one of the key technologies, high-speed access, is not a focus of legislation? We need a renewed spotlight on the advantages of leading the world in technology innovation and improving high-speed access for everyone if we are going to compete in the race for high-speed connectivity. As of January 2022, only 62.5 percent of the global population has broadband.

> *We're now seeing the intersection of physical and virtual work worlds, driven by generational, societal, and technology changes. Add globalization to the mix, and there's an increased need for significantly improved workforce collaboration to drive innovation.*
>
> —Dan Fallon, former vice president and chief technology officer, Navistar

MINIMUM COMPUTING REQUIREMENTS

In today's companies, computers are the workhorses of all departments, connecting the workers, assisting with work creation and completion, and providing information anytime, anywhere. The same is true in a virtual environment, where workers connect to grid computers, mainframes, or the cloud.

In a virtualized world with a global workforce, cloud-based platforms have changed how companies deploy software, allowing workers to tap into the computing power they need to work effectively from anywhere. These cloud-based platforms make it easier to secure, manage, and scale workers from an IT perspective. IT departments are welcoming the cloud technology with open arms as it becomes the next extension to personal computers and mobile devices.

COLLABORATION

Collaboration is the new medium for information exchange in the cloud, and now, more than ever, technological advances in collaboration are driving a virtual, global economy. The next-generation workforce will require virtual collaboration skills to participate in group or team projects. Their individual contributions can be used independently or packaged together and reassembled as part of a group or team effort.

Collaboration and communication tools can now take the place of face-to-face meetings, phone calls, and even email. These tools are dramatically different than they were a decade ago, and now they are a staple in every office environment, whether physical or virtual. Webcasts, web-conferencing, and webinars have opened the door for a decentralized workforce that can work from anywhere.

THE CLOUD

Cloud computing is not the revolution; it is the evolution of what started almost twenty years ago, and now start-up organizations are relying on the cloud for unimaginable amounts of computing power, without any capital expense. Imagine being able to process hundreds of millions or billions of knowledge scans or searches without owning any technology infrastructure.

You can hardly look at an IT strategy document today without seeing mention of cloud computing, even though it has been around for years. So why all the attention? The model has now crossed the chasm to penetrate corporate America, which traditionally relied on internal infrastructure. This is a significant shift in IT mindset in what will certainly be remembered as a disruptive technology strategy that changed the way the world works, literally.

MOBILE

We would not do the book justice without focusing on mobile devices. Smartphones and tablets are changing the world at a greater pace than the adoption of any technology prior to their existence. Connected to high-speed access and the cloud, they are fast becoming the standard for staying connected in a virtual world.

Smartphones and tablets are changing the world at a greater pace than the adoption of any technology prior to their existence.

Remember we mentioned that anyone with a smartphone can change the way they work? You now have the tools to monetize your value, your skills, or your experience in a virtual environment.

Want to hear a staggering statistic? According to GSM Association real-time intelligence data, there are now over 10.57 billion mobile connections worldwide, which surpasses the current world population of 7.93 billion implied by UN digital analyst estimates.[21] This data means there are 2.64 billion more mobile connections than people worldwide.

Understand how the cloud and mobile devices are changing the way we live, and you will recognize how the new world of work will empower the worker and change the way the world works.

THE NEW ASSEMBLY LINE

What happened when Henry Ford changed the way automobiles were manufactured? His ingenious business model, which included paying workers wages that allowed them to purchase these horseless carriages, created built-in customers to buy his automobiles. This turned Ford's laborers into satisfied new customers, forever changing the way the world of commerce operates.

Technology is the key to creating the new assembly line in today's workplace. Virtual work platforms that remove all boundaries between the type of work offered and the type of work accepted are the key to ensuring we don't try to over-manage virtual talent and thereby kill the very spirit of it.

Think about what happens when companies compete for talent. Basically, in a no-boundaries world, the worker literally punches into work they find satisfying as long as the compensation is proportionate with the value of their output. The worker is empowered, and technology enables more freedom by ensuring the *work* is managed, rather than the worker. This type of thinking, which is aided by technology rather than management, will increase the fractionalization of work, and thereby increase the pool of workers.

---

21   "Over Half World's Population Now Using Mobile Internet," GSMA, September 28, 2021, https://www.gsma.com/newsroom/press-release/over-half-worlds-population-now-using-mobile-internet/.

We noticed the move toward a boundary-less world over the last decade. In the beginning, it was only something large companies could afford. Today, finding the best talent globally is becoming as common as searching for a highly recommended restaurant online. Today, it's clearly more efficient for companies to hire talent online, regardless of their location.

—Alex George, president and chief
product officer, Emplify

JUST GOOGLE IT

There is no better example of how to succeed in the new world of work than Google. The legend of how Larry Page and Sergey Brin invented an entire industry based on searching the Internet has become entrepreneurial lore.

Google doesn't share its search volume data. However, it's estimated as of June 2021, Google processes approximately 63,000 search queries every second, translating to 5.6 billion searches per day and approximately two trillion global searches per year. The average person conducts between three and four searches each day. What Google unknowingly created was technology-enabled access to information that continues to power the new work machine.

Companies that pioneer new ways of empowering virtual workers will win, while professionals who find their passions and market them in the new world of work will ultimately rule. To take full advantage of the fractionalization of work, be prepared to try new ways of working and new ways of living.

As more and more companies adopt similar models and expand their labor reach globally, the cascading effect will become an accelerant for every organization to embrace the model or face irrelevance and extinction. The empowered worker will challenge the status quo of yesterday's organization and raise the bar on performance, creating frightening competition for organizations that fail to adapt.

What Does the Future Hold?

First, the world has no boundaries, and everything is global. Anyone or any company with value to offer can market goods or services anywhere in the world with a click of a mouse or on a mobile device. Individuals can contribute using collaboration tools. Today's networks provide the horsepower to enable group-work and crowdsourcing. Seamless communication across all channels, combined with the virtualization of most forward-thinking teams, creates an entire new organizational model.

In the new world of work, we like to think of this as the next organizational hierarchy, and it exhibits powerful contrasts: technology is changing so rapidly that it is increasing the efficiency of all organizations while empowering customers, as noted in chapter 4. Customers are very different today than they were just a decade ago: they are more informed, and they learn, live, work, and play differently, aided by new technology.

While business is changing with technology, it's important to remember that your customer looks very different today and is being changed by the same information revolution. In the next chapter, we'll show you how to capitalize on the needs of the new customer.

CHAPTER 14

No Buildings, No Fear

Way back before the turn of the new millennium (which seems like eons ago), we saw that the world was changing. It was clear that technology would transform the way people worked.

In fact, working in a virtual environment is not new; it began in the early 1970s, when technology first started to link offices together to the headquarters office. Known as telework or telecommuting back then, companies first started to realize the benefit of a virtual workforce almost fifty years ago. By decentralizing the workforce, people could work from anywhere, and by leveraging technology, work could be joined together with applications and groupware.

So why did it take so long to understand the benefits? The main culprit was the employers' fear that they would lose control over the workforce. So why does working from someplace that is not a traditional office make some managers so uncomfortable? It has to do with our management's need to see the workers and what they do, a need for *control*.

Society also created a barrier from a psychological standpoint rooted in our human need for belonging and routine; it's the same reason people stay in a bad relationship or job—habit!

> *The reality is that the world has simply changed and letting go of control is part of that. Even if you're a manager, you have to let go and let people do their jobs, especially in a virtual environment.*
>
> —Jeanne Jones, global director, Indeed

Beyond the Four Walls

Increasingly, companies are using freelance workers to fulfill their needs, thereby enhancing flexibility so they can expand or shrink depending on demand. The new contingent workforce is laying the groundwork for the new virtual corporation that is no longer tied to the office building. The cost benefit allows employers to tap into an experienced, educated workforce on demand, as needed, to support project work and seasonal growth spikes.

In order to fully leverage the new workforce, companies should address the advantages and disadvantages of why this new workforce is emerging.

ADVANTAGES	
EMPLOYER	**WORKER**
Flex staffing	Flexibility of hours
Reduced overhead	Work remotely
No benefits	Variable work
Scale	Variety
Improved margin	More opportunities
Specialty expertise as needed	Projects you choose
No labor unions	Less job discontent
Variable labor model	Self-employment
DISADVANTAGES	
EMPLOYER	**WORKER**
No loyalty	Limited job security
Less retention	Minimal benefits
Lost domain knowledge	Cyclical wages
Challenging social aspects	Less career advancement

Even considering these disadvantages, the advantages are still tilting the scales to a new virtual contingent workforce, creating a mutually beneficial relationship between the employer and worker. And there is no longer a stigma attached to working in this capacity.

In the late 1990s, while working at GE TechTeam, a joint venture between General Electric and TechTeam, Tim saw the first signs of how the new world of work model had evolved to the point of efficiency that could not be stopped.

GE TechTeam serviced large Fortune 100 companies for technical support and warranty management, focusing mostly on the call center troubleshooting and break-fix transactions associated with warranty support for the computer industry. Every fourth quarter, we would start hiring staff in October, knowing we would not need the support until after Thanksgiving, with the volumes peaking after Christmas until the end of the third week of January.

Since 60–70 percent of the support volume would come during that timeframe, a steady-state workforce was not needed year round. The biggest challenge was recruiting staff for the peak periods, knowing the pink slips would be issued in late January.

Now, with the GE TechTeam example fresh in your mind, how does the new model look now? The benefits are undeniable; using the nation as your recruiting pool and targeted selection for recruiting the specialized skill set, a variable staffing model could have solved the challenges we had every fourth quarter or any seasonal staffing challenges.

Today, the cloud helps us deliver the same connectivity and productivity you would find in a brick-and-mortar office. The entrepreneurial spirit has surfaced, and the new professionals earn respect working for themselves in fields they are passionate about and on their own terms.

LEGISLATION

Ironically, the new world of work has nothing to do with national governments, because it was created by innovative entrepreneurs who saw a need to connect talent with companies that needed fractional/ virtual workers, and they created platforms to make that happen.

The challenge is that they inadvertently created a work movement so strong that it now threatens the corporate culture of our country.

A big challenge with the new gig workforce is the difference in categorizing an employee and an independent contractor. In 2020, Uber was sued in a class action lawsuit claiming their drivers should be employees with benefits and not independent contractors. A number of other gig-staffed companies have also faced lawsuits seeking to force them to convert their contractors to employees, which carries a host of tax, wage, and job benefit costs. The argument over misclassification of workers will continue for the foreseeable future, making it more important to follow federal and state rules.

The US is not prepared for the change. Political parties are divided. Culturally, we are conditioned to working in the cube,

The new world of work is about results, performance, and competing for work. In many cases, it's the antithesis of our old way of work distribution.

receiving praise for doing what we're told, being granted health benefits because we're inside the corporation, and collecting a check every two weeks. The new world of work is about results, performance, and competing for work. In many cases, it's the antithesis of our old way of work distribution.

COUNTING HEADS

Currently, only jobs added as employees are considered part of the workforce by the US Bureau of Labor Statistics (BLS). The agency refers on its site to contract work as an "alternative employment arrangement." It defines the contingent worker as follows: "Contingent workers are persons who do not expect their jobs to last or who reported that their jobs are temporary."[22]

Contingent workers do not have an implicit or explicit contract for ongoing employment. Alternative employment arrangements include persons employed as independent contractors, on-call workers, temporary help agency workers, and workers provided by contract firms.

In order to advance the model and progress, we must have legislation that supports a society and individuals who innovate and create. That new legislation should include new classification systems that give contract workers their due by making them part of the American workforce. And new laws should be enacted to bring contract workers under the protective umbrella of US law.

As a publication from the National Employment Law Project, *Organizing for Workplace Equity: Model State Legislation for Nonstandard Workers*, notes, "Despite strong public support for nonstandard workers, the nation's employment laws have not kept pace with the growth in nonstandard work… Thus, nonstandard workers lack some of the most basic protections of labor and employment laws that apply to permanent, full-time employees."[23]

The basis of the new workforce is that workers choose the "lifestyle" career because it meets their monetary and personal objectives, mainly freedom. Federal laws need to recognize the validity of this choice and count independent contractors and sole proprietorship businesses as part of job-growth statistics.

---

22   "Contingent and Alternative Employment Arrangements Summary," US Bureau of Labor Statistics, June 7, 2018, https://www.bls.gov/news.release/conemp.nr0.htm.

23   Maurice Emsellen and Catherine Ruckelshaus, "Organizing for Workplace Equity: Model State Legislation for 'Nonstandard' Workers," National Employment Law Project, November 2000, https://s27147.pcdn.co/wp-content/uploads/2015/03/Organizing-for-Workplace-Equity-Model-State-Legislation-for-Nonstandard.pdf.

The old-school method for counting jobs should be updated to measure reality. We need to provide an environment and culture to foster the virtual entrepreneurial spirit of the new contingent workforce.

Legislation needs to allow Virtualpreneurs to be counted as part of the employment numbers. The support for the independent business owner will help us create jobs, strengthen the economy, and get us working again.

Time or Money?

Yahoo! Finance and *Parade* magazine teamed up for a job satisfaction / happiness survey conducted in the second quarter of 2012 to discover how Americans view their careers, jobs, work environments, and futures. One of the key findings in the job happiness poll was that more than 60 percent of Americans would go back and rewrite their careers.[24] Think about that for a second.

> **Almost two-thirds of the people who make up the American workforce would hit the rewind button and start their careers over.**

Almost two-thirds of the people who make up the American workforce would hit the rewind button and start their careers over.

Why would the majority of working Americans want a redo? This is an important question in the new world of work because it leads to another critical question: How can we increase job satisfaction? The answer is to move the work to the cloud, fractionalize the work, and

---

24 "Job Happiness Poll: Most Americans Wish They Could Hit Reset Button on Their Careers," *Parade*, August 31, 2012, https://parade.com/49725/parade/job-happiness-poll-americans-wish-hit-reset-button-on-careers/.

develop a compensation-based structure for performance and quality. Hard work and creativity should be rewarded based on individual contribution and as part of a team working toward a common goal or objective.

The most disturbing statistic from the study is that more than 35 percent said they would fire their bosses. Is this because of the absence of managerial talent and leadership in today's business? Perhaps. But it does suggest that embarking on a self-directed, conscious career choice of working as a Virtualpreneur in a career that you are passionate about will lead to increased economic output and job satisfaction.

Mercer Research conducted a study in late 2011 concluding that millennial-generation employees (those born after 1982) are 50 percent more likely to leave their jobs because they do not believe they are in a "sound place to work."[25] So, that means more than 50 percent of the younger generation is looking for a better alternative.

The most compelling confirmation of the new world of work model is that two out of every three Americans would like to improve their workspaces. These findings corroborate the need for the next-generation workforce that chooses the task/work product, sets the compensation structure based on a perfect market system, and essentially works independently wherever they have access to the Internet. It also lays the groundwork for having world-class technology available for this workforce.

What does the contingent workforce feel is relevant to its well-being? The answer is job satisfaction, pure and simple. When you were in grammar school, you were probably given very specific reasons why you needed to learn each subject and how the information would be

---

25 Haig Nalbantian and Tauseef Rahman, "Separating Fact from Fiction about Millennials at Work," Mercer, April 23, 2019, https://www.mercer.us/our-thinking/career/separating-fact-from-fiction-about-millennials-at-work.html.

applied in the future. Did all the knowledge you gained turn out to be useful, or did it simply point you in the direction of a traditional career?

What happens when the rules change? What happens when you learn a different way or gain a specific knowledge that you are passionate about somewhere other than a traditional school? Can you begin to break through the confines of what society has dictated to you and allow yourself to create and innovate? Yes. All you need is a computer or mobile device and the Internet. Can you compete now? You bet you can.

The bottom line is that the four walls that once kept workers captive are gone. Over the last decade, technological and social changes have given rise to new, borderless business models. That means you, as a professional or business manager, have ultimate freedom. But here's the rub: You're now competing with a world full of other professionals.

Are you ready for this? Are you ready to *compete* for work? The global talent pool is, and they are not working in an office. Companies around the world are betting that Americans can't compete in a global talent marketplace without boundaries. Are you ready to prove them wrong?

Now that the world has opened up a global talent pool with no boundaries, what do you think will be next? What industries will benefit from virtualization?

CHAPTER 15

Everything Is Digital

Everything in business and life is now digital, and lines between the physical and virtual continue to blur at an unfathomable rate.

The new world of work has fundamentally shifted how businesses operate—providing employees with a real-time, constant stream of emails, messages, and digital communications. In a report posted by Canadian-based company Deloitte, researchers observed that "as the distinction between professional and personal life dissolves, and the workplace becomes truly digital, employees are communicating and collaborating in unprecedented ways."[26]

Social posting and real-time updates have virtually no boundaries or geographical restrictions. *What should I post today? What platform should I use to communicate my message? Should I tell people what I had*

---

26 "The Digital Workplace: Think, Share, Do," Deloitte, April 2014, https://www2.deloitte. com/content/dam/Deloitte/be/Documents/technology/The_digital_workplace_ Deloitte.pdf.

for breakfast? Do I write about where my family is traveling this week? These are the questions social media users grapple with each day.

Common information individuals previously wouldn't have considered sharing with people outside their close social circle, they now freely distribute to hundreds, thousands, and even millions of people. In fact, social status is now determined by how many people you can influence. And often, these updates are not limited to one social network circle of influence, and a message shared on one channel can be shared with the friends of numerous networks.

Consider for a moment the rise of digital technology in the past thirty years. Unlike previous generations in world history that saw little technological or innovative advancement from one generation to the next, the last few decades have brought our world closer together than ever before. Video conversations with virtually any person of our choosing can take place around the globe. And this is just the beginning.

Adapt or Die

A decade ago, we wrote in our first edition of *The New World of Work* that we were undertaking a massive transition from the cube to the cloud. We shared how it was our belief that in the next few years, the workforce would shift and give way to a new generation of entrepreneurs that saw the value of having teams work in remote locations. Admittedly, this declaration was met with much resistance. "You can't have people just work at home," employers said. "They'll be too distracted, slack on their work, and pull the unity of an organization apart."

But two years of the COVID-19 pandemic revealed just how misplaced these criticisms were. To the surprise of many business owners, the forced shift to remote work actually increased productivity within companies. The pandemic changed the way we looked at established realities of business such as an office. With many shifting to virtual workspaces, the need for a physical location became unnecessary. The same technology that blended our professional and personal lives now allows us to do our jobs from home or anywhere in the world.

The problem is that humans can be stubborn and creatures of habit. We like to do and live in ways that feel comfortable. Few leaders thought they would live to see the day when most of their team did not come into an office from nine to five. But for many, this is precisely what has happened. They did not welcome this shift. But it was thrust upon them, and they were faced with that age old conundrum: adapt or die.

As we have stated for years, work has been fractionalized, talent has been globalized, and technology has been virtualized, paving the way for the new world of work—a digital world shared with real-world artificial intelligence. And contrary to what many predict, AI, robotics, and automation are not going to destroy jobs. Instead, they are going to create new opportunities—the same way technology has done with every wave of innovation. There is a massive labor shortage today, and real-world AI in a digital world will be a welcome addition to the new, digital workforce.

Life-changing as this cube-to-cloud revolution was, there is an even greater shift that entrepreneurs of the next decade will face. It is coming, and it will absolutely impact the way they live and do business. And their ability to adapt to this digital change will determine whether their businesses will survive or die.

A NEW, DIGITAL WAY TO WORK

Many executives think that owning a smartphone or moving away from paper files to digital receipts implies they are current with technological trends. But for the entrepreneur that plans to be in business for more than five years, they must understand that the level of human and artificial intelligence interaction will increase at an even more rapid rate than digital transitions of the past. The digital revolution will gain momentum and speed as the digital trends of tomorrow will far surpass the speed and size of innovations from the past.

Artificial intelligence, automation, and robotic process automation are taking the place of traditional jobs at an unprecedented rate. "The pace of change is accelerating," researchers conclude. "Competition for the right talent is fierce. And 'talent' no longer means the same as ten years ago; many of the roles, skills and job titles of tomorrow are unknown to us today."[27] On the other hand, jobs that are not lost now have digital assistance from AI and automation, improving deliverables, timeframes, and outcomes.

Just as a surfer cannot stop the waves in an ocean, a business owner in this digital era cannot stand against the digital tsunami headed their way.

If organizations are going to survive in the coming decade, they must recognize the emerging patterns of the digital workforce, understand the impact these changes will have on their teams and customers, and then take proactive steps to work *with* rather than *against* these changes in current. Just as a

---

27   PwC, "Workforce of the Future: The Competing Forces Shaping 2030," April 8, 2017, https://www.pwc.com/gx/en/services/people-organisation/workforce-of-the-future/workforce-of-the-future-the-competing-forces-shaping-2030-pwc.pdf.

surfer cannot stop the waves in an ocean, a business owner in this digital era cannot stand against the digital tsunami headed their way.

This chapter was the premise for Tim's next book focusing on the digital, intelligent workforce and how we will work with AI and robotics in the new, digital world of work.

Instead of pushing against the waves, leaders must learn to adapt, ride the waves, and use them to their advantage. More importantly, education *must* change.

SECTION 5

Now What?

CHAPTER 16

Education Must Change (or Die)

Beyond predicting the workforce transformation fueled by the gig economy, the other revolution we saw on the horizon was education. We knew that education must change because just as the workforce goes, so goes education.

Although COVID-19 revealed the inevitable—you don't need to be physically in a classroom to learn—what is also now clear is that the role higher education plays in career planning is less important than knowing who you are, what you want, and why you're here.

For the United States or any nation to compete in this new world of work, one long-standing institution must transform: that institution is education.

America's colleges and universities are in the best position to assist corporations in equipping young workers with the skills to capitalize on the new world of work—if these institutions can themselves learn to think differently.

Three unique strategies are evolving specifically to address the challenge of renovating the workforce through education. These are:

1. **Strategy 1:** Focus on the trades. Many young adults can create a sustainable income by skipping college and building a career in the trades. This long-standing model is back in vogue and for very good reason.

2. **Strategy 2:** Adapt the collegiate degree system. There are some leaders who think our entire post-secondary educational system is flawed. They point to Steve Jobs, Michael Dell, and Mark Zuckerberg, wildly successful entrepreneurs who never graduated from college yet were lifelong learners who created transformative products, companies, and business models. An emerging trend is occurring *between* business and higher education that yields incredible promise.

3. **Strategy 3:** Focus on why, not what. Most college programs focus on a career rather than purpose. Yet the generation graduating high school today is not motivated by money. They are motivated by meaning.

Strategy 1: Focus on the Trades

Since the pandemic, millions of students delayed college, opting to work instead. Two-year public schools were the hardest hit. Conversely, skilled-trades programs across the country, especially associate degree programs in fields like HVAC and automotive repair, saw enrollment numbers swell.

How community college enrollment shifted during the pandemic

Percent change in undergraduate enrollment, by major, from 2019 to 2021. Programs with the highest enrollment or with notable changes shown.

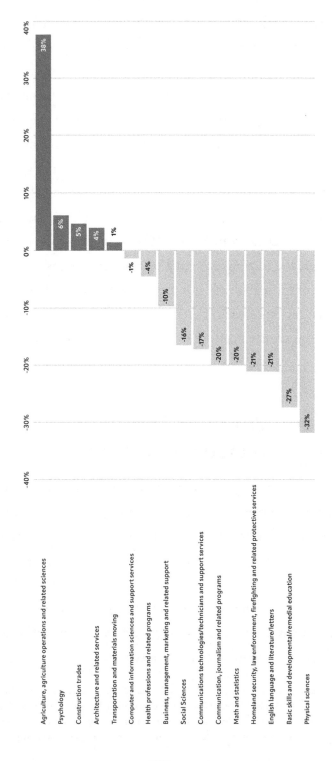

Furthermore, a growing number of people without a bachelor's degree are outearning their four-year college peers, according to a study from Georgetown University's Center on Education and the Workforce. The study found that in the years 2017 through 2019, on average, 16 percent of high school graduates, 23 percent of workers with some college, and 28 percent of associate-degree holders earned *more money* than half of all workers with a bachelor's degree.[28]

For students who don't have access to a career or college counselor, there are a number of helpful resources for making post-high school decisions. The US Bureau of Labor Statistics offers tools to help people understand the earning potential of different careers.

One of those tools, the Occupational Outlook Handbook, classifies career options based on average pay, the level of education needed, and how much the profession is expected to grow over the next ten years.

Strategy 2: Adapt the Collegiate Degree System

New, virtual university models have been evolving since the University of Phoenix was created by Dr. John Sterling in 1976. Most accredited colleges use virtual formats, and the rest were forced to do so during COVID-19. On the surface, it might seem like this is the answer. But is it?

What we saw ten years ago, which is even more clear today, is that the four-year college degree system doesn't match the needs of businesses or the workforce of tomorrow.

---

28   Anthony Carnevale, Stephen Rose, and Ban Cheah, "The College Payoff: Education, Occupation, Lifetime Earnings," Georgetown University, accessed October 26, 2022, https://cew.georgetown.edu/wp-content/uploads/collegepayoff-completed.pdf.

At the time we wrote the first edition of *The New World of Work*, major educational institutions had begun to experiment with new ideas to approach education differently. We saw things like:

- Empowered, a professional certificate program by UCLA, using its higher education resources within organizations for workforce training. What Empowered understood was the learn-as-you-go culture that is the basis of the new world of work. Since then, over one hundred respected universities have modified their structures to include professional certification programs as part of their core curriculum.

- Free online courses by world-class institutions have been an incubation lab leveraged by most large university brands. Powered by Coursera and Khan Academy, top-tier research universities, from Harvard to Stanford, have introduced learners to the power of great thought. Having access to great thought is the basis of the new world of work, and this new delivery model could fuel technological innovation and economic growth.

We believed then, and are certain now, that the educational infrastructure needs to adapt more than simply creating virtual courses. The real challenge with migrating college curriculum to an online format is that it doesn't get to the root of the problem. Whereas online higher education made sense decades ago, in the

Whereas online higher education made sense decades ago, in the new world of work, the college degree itself is now in question—not merely the delivery format.

new world of work, the college degree itself is now in question—not merely the delivery format.

Today, new workers are intuitively self-educated and notoriously driven by a "learn as you go" culture fed by YouTube and Google. They don't want to learn *anything* they don't need to know (which is the basis of most collegiate systems), because they know they will learn it … *when they need it.* This is based on their understanding that in the Information Revolution, knowledge is at their fingertips.

A college education of any type was once regarded as a first-class ticket to a better life. However, the rising costs of higher education, as well as the burden of student loans and a rapidly changing job market, have left many wondering: Is college really worth it?

For specialty degrees, most studies have confirmed an ROI for a college degree.

A recent study from the Foundation for Research on Equal Opportunity (FREOPP) laid the value proposition of various college degree programs out plainly. The report showed how the ROI varies across almost thirty thousand different bachelor-degree programs.

Specialty degrees, such as engineering, computer science, nursing, etc., produced an ROI of over $1 million. However, the more generic degrees, such as art, music, and psychology, had a zero or even negative net financial value.[29] In other words, earning a bachelor's degree in some studies could leave a young adult worse off financially than if that professional had not gone to college at all.

What is clear is that for professionals to compete in the new world of work, something has to change about the way we educate our future workforce.

---

29   Preston Cooper, "Is College Worth It? A Comprehensive Return on Investment Analysis," FREOPP.org (Medium, October 19, 2022), https://freopp.org/is-college-worth-it-a-comprehensive-return-on-investment-analysis-1b2ad17f84c8.

Strategy 3: Focus on Why, Not What

The biggest challenge with educational institutions is they are built on the fundamental question of, "What do you want to be when you grow up?" versus a more soulful question of why it matters in the first place.

More than following passions, purpose is the soul food of the next generation. It sets them on a path that fuels their sense of belonging, their willingness to work hard, and their desire to commit to a path. Some executives view this generation as unmotivated, when in reality, they are driven by an invisible force: purpose.

Tech company Cognizant found 93 percent of Gen Z workers across all countries believe that feeling like they belong at work is important and "creating personal connections with managers and coworkers is an important part of belonging."

More and more businesses are aligning their purpose to that of those they recruit, yet colleges have yet to understand how to maximize purpose to fuel enrollment. It's one of those *Where's Waldo?* exercises, where the answer is right under their nose. Yet they can't, or won't, see it.

Private organizations have built large platforms matching professionals to their sense of purpose over the last decade. Ironically, what COVID-19 did was showcase the power of meaning, as the Great Resignation was powered by workers making professional choices based on meaning over money.

The best part is that there continues to be a different breed of company that understands the power of purpose and has successfully matched workers to a meaningful career inside their organization. This new way of work will frame the entire next decade as we enter the Purpose Revolution.

CHAPTER 17

Business and Purpose: Find Your Why

Globalization is no longer about evil corporate executives outsourcing jobs or governmental policies favoring offshoring. In fact, it never really was about those things. Jobs are being crowdsourced on virtual work platforms regardless of what governments legislate or corporations create. There are no boundaries.

The most important question for businesses and professionals attempting to navigate the new world of work isn't where we are going, but why it matters in the first place.

As the world changes, one thing remains the same: we are all seeking more meaning in our lives, our careers, and our businesses.

Businesses that want to compete for talent in the new world of work marketplace must have a clear answer as to why they matter.

In 2006, a few business leaders started with the idea that a different kind of economy was not only possible, but necessary—and that business could lead the way toward a new, stakeholder-driven model. B Lab became known for certifying B Corporations, which are companies that meet high standards of social and environmental performance, accountability, and transparency. Today, B Lab is the nonprofit network transforming the global economy to benefit all people, communities, and the planet.

The B Lab movement was followed by Conscious Capitalism, which is a philosophy based on the belief that a new form of capital holds the potential for enhancing corporate performance while simultaneously serving the greater good. Conscious Capitalism focuses on four pillars of strategy, starting with defining an organization's higher purpose.

What's even more exciting is that the most recent Global Entrepreneurship Monitor Annual Report found that the motivator for most new entrepreneurs is now *"to make a difference in the world."*

Nine economies reported that three out of five of those starting and running a new business agreed that "to make a difference in the world" was their primary motivation. Making a difference in the world suggests that social, cultural, or environmental objectives are driving entrepreneurial behavior. Specifically, the majority of the entrepreneurial population from Europe, North America, Latin America, and the Caribbean said they were motivated to create a business to "make a difference in the world" versus only to "build wealth or very high income."

This statistic is not to be ignored. The majority of new entrepreneurs now say that their primary motivation for their business is to make a difference.

> *Yanik Silver, Author of* Evolved Enterprise *noted that within the next decade, terms like* conscious capitalism, triple bottom line, for-benefit companies, *and* evolved enterprise *will no longer be used to describe unusual, impactful companies—because they'll simply be referred to as* businesses.

This means that *conscious business will be the best way to do business. Period.*

In 2020, during the pandemic, Terri founded a business growth platform for conscious brands to learn how to expand and grow their businesses using conscious business practices.

Conscious business will be the best way to do business. Period.

Today, Shift/Co has already helped hundreds of conscious businesses in eleven different countries establish a firm foundation for scalable success. Almost 80 percent of the businesses using Shift/Co's methods doubled or tripled their revenue within one to two years of joining the platform.

Terri believes the success of Shift/Co is rooted in purpose. These businesses have a reason for existing and a plan to create change—both of which fuel both their passion, and their growth.

Purpose is a definitive statement about the difference a business makes in the world. Shift/Co's members are all purpose-based businesses—entrepreneurs who are building something to make the world better and make money.

If a company has a purpose and can articulate it with clarity and passion, workers are better able to understand *why* the company exists and how they can add value. Management is aligned, designs are clear, employees know why their business matters, and everyone is clear about how to achieve the purpose. When companies find employees aligned with that purpose, they are intrinsically passionate about the work.

With the new world of work, businesses can source talent from virtually anywhere. On one hand, it may seem as if the business has the power. However, the real benefit of the new world of work is that talent can find work anywhere. There are no boundaries to job searches, and you can literally pick up projects globally. The best talent, both salaried and contract, will be attracted to companies that have a clear sense of purpose—a clear why.

It is because of this revolutionary shift that it is imperative to find your why. It is mission-critical for companies to know why they exist and how their business serves.

In this book we have tried to outline real solutions to this brave new world and have encouraged a new way of thinking about public education, corporate talent strategies, and work management.

In the new age, most jobs will be contractors or temps, and self-employment will become the norm. This requires governments capable of articulating this new strategy and a pioneering group of companies and leaders that can chart the course for the new way of work.

It is because of this revolutionary shift that it is imperative to find your why. It is mission-critical for companies to know why they exist and how their business serves.

There are several excellent examples of great companies—some of which are clients of ours—that have identified their purpose and reiterate that purpose in everything they do.

Professionals and Purpose

For professionals, you too must find your why. You must know your purpose. Your purpose is who you are, whereas your job is just what you do. Evaluating strengths and passions forms the basis of a purpose statement. At what do you truly excel? What are you passionate about? How does it serve?

The more clearly you understand your purpose—your why—the easier it will be to evaluate work opportunities as you chart your path in the new world of work.

> *Purpose isn't something you do.*
> *Purpose is who you are.*
>
> —Terri Maxwell

Your purpose was the same when you were six years old and was what probably attracted you to a particular field of study in college. If most of us had been left alone to follow our passions, our careers would have looked dramatically different. Your purpose will be the same when you die. The question is whether or not we will live our purpose in between our life and our death.

Purpose is your personal and professional why. It's who you are, and it's what you're meant to bring to the world. It's your unique gift, and it can be the best compass for charting a path in this new world of work.

Now What?

In the 1930s, jobs moved from the farm to the factory. Today, work as we know it has migrated once again, only this time it has moved from the cube to the cloud.

In the new world of work, there are no limitations to what, how, or where work can be performed. This new world has spawned an entire new way of organizing work and is responsible for innovative business models and career opportunities, all with one thing in common—no boundaries. The world is your workforce!

The new world of work has leveraged the Information Revolution to transform work and move it from the cube to the cloud. As a result, your business has been transformed, and if you don't develop a strategy to compete for this talent and develop a clear sense of corporate purpose, the best talent will go elsewhere. So, corporate executives, the new world of work has transformed talent strategies. The question is, Have you transformed your business to capitalize on this new world?

Professionals: As a result of the new world of work, your career has been transformed. The question is, Have you been transformed? Will you continue to search for jobs the old way or chart new career strategies to maximize your purpose and create roles you can be passionate about? Are you looking for the jobs you lost, or are you reinventing yourselves to maximize this new world?

In the new world of work, there are no boundaries. There are only opportunities. They may appear different—and possibly scarier—than those of the past because they *are* different. However, they don't have to be scary, not when you're prepared.

The companies and professionals that maximize a boundary-less world of work will be able to teach and lead because they are not afraid of moving ahead.

We hope this book has helped you understand and appreciate our continuing and thrilling leap into the future. If you—as either a professional or business owner—embrace the new world of work, you are destined to become one of its leading citizens.

ABOUT THE AUTHORS

Tim Houlne is the CEO of Humach (Humans and Machines), one of the leading customer experience providers focusing on artificial intelligence with humans in the loop. He is the former CEO of Working Solutions, one of the original pioneers of the virtual, work-at-home contact center providers. Tim is also presently the chairman of Humach Jamaica. He recently joined as a member of the Forbes Technology Council. He has served on several boards, including Vision Bank of Texas (acquired by Texas Bank and Trust), Golfinity, Swivl, Buon Vino, Imprinted, and the Movie Institute. He previously was an Ernst & Young Entrepreneur of the Year finalist.

Tim has been a futurist and authored multiple articles and white papers covering a wide range of subjects on remote workforce, digital transformation, technology enablement, cloud adoption, and managed platforms as services. He is a highly sought-after speaker for industry conferences, business summits, and schools. He is committed to helping others embrace new concepts and ideas that improve the lives of working professionals while ensuring excellent bottom-line results. His collaboration on this book is the latest example of that commitment.

Terri Maxwell is the founder and CEO of Share On Purpose, Inc. and a business cultivator who created six innovative brands using her Conscious Business Growth Platform. She also started a speculator fund to invest in social ventures focused on making the world better. In an entrepreneurial career that spans almost thirty years, Terri has launched, owned, sold, rebranded, or turned around more than fifty brands. Her latest concept is Shift/Co, a business growth platform for conscious entrepreneurs. Her first company, Succeed On Purpose, has offered training to Virtualpreneurs since 2013.

Terri is known for her game-changing models for both business and personal success. Her work has been featured in the *New York Times*, *Success* magazine, FOX, and CBS. She is an Outlive Yourself Award recipient and was named Small Business Mentor of the Year by the National Association of Women Business Owners. She is the author of *Succeed on Purpose: Everything Happens for a Reason* and the coauthor of *The New World of Work: From the Cube to the Cloud*.

9 781642 258318